ADAM SMITH
AND THE ORIGINS OF
AMERICAN
ENTERPRISE

Also by Roy C. Smith

The Wealth Creators

Comeback: The Restoration of American Banking Power
in the New World Economy

The Money Wars

The Global Bankers

WITH INGO WALTER

High Finance in the Euro-Zone: Competing in the
New European Capital Market

Street Smarts

ADAM SMITH AND THE ORIGINS OF AMERICAN ENTERPRISE

How America's Industrial Success
Was Forged by the Timely Ideas
of a Brilliant Scots Economist

ROY C. SMITH

T·T

TRUMAN TALLEY BOOKS
ST. MARTIN'S PRESS
NEW YORK

www.stmartins.com

ISBN 0-312-28552-3

First Edition: December 2002

10   9   8   7   6   5   4   3   2   1

CONTENTS

INTRODUCTION

The physical reality of our economic circumstances at the time of the American Revolution was quite daunting. We were tiny, a country of less than three million people spread out over a narrow strip of land from Maine to Georgia. We had lived as British dependents for 150 years and had not developed much beyond Britain's image of us as a principal supplier of raw materials and a promising customer for its manufactured goods. We had hardly any manufacturing, no banks or financial resources, and were exhausted and depleted by nearly eight long years of war and revolution. Future growth seemed possible only by the backbreaking effort of clearing and settling more of the ar.

wilderness on the frontier, and that would depend on having the people to do it, but the country had no people to spare.

These conditions established limits and highlighted the country's deficiencies that would have to be overcome for its economy to grow. If it did not grow, and grow at a greater rate than during colonial times, there was doubt that the country could survive. If the American people thought they would be worse off as an independent nation, they might call the British king back in, as the British Parliament did after the death of Oliver Cromwell in 1660. Or, if the economy never developed, and even if its citizens preferred independence, the country might not be able to defend itself against some sort of foreign invasion.

Another factor, an intake of ideas and philosophies for governing and developing the new United States, was also of enormous importance. We know that it was, because the American government has lasted—only little changed—for more than two hundred years despite enormous shifts in the size, scope, and complexity of the country. No other country has ever had a similar experience of forging a democratic republic. Few have started from such a poorly developed base of economic institutions or infrastructure. Men with no experience of either government or economics cut the entire plan for civil government and economic development out of whole cloth. Most of these men did not possess any outstanding credentials or skills. Few were saints or geniuses; all were men of action, prone to weaknesses and mistakes. Yet their work of nation-building has not only held, it has strengthened through continuous use. The intellectual inflows the founders received were many. These came mainly from a Europe bursting with new ideas about almost everything that affected the way men live. This was the Enlightenment, a period of great awakening in science, religion, the arts, and government. Many of these ideas and theories were seen to be useful in America and were put to use by its founding fathers. Among such ideas, none had more impact than those of Adam Smith, the author in 1776 of *The Wealth of Nations* and the father of modern economic science.

Adam Smith is not well known in the United States beyond the field of economics. Many recognize his name, however, and might associate him with an "invisible hand," or the principles of "laissez-faire," under which a government's obligation is not to interfere with the natural workings of markets. Adam Smith was by training and profession a moral philosopher, and what he had to say about economics was almost entirely deduced by him from his general observation of the commercial life going on around him and his understanding of the history of men and their affairs, going back to the Romans. He did not make experiments or models, nor did he collect large amounts of data as economists do today. Mostly, he thought about things abstractly, as Einstein did, and simply formed his conclusions about economic life and prosperity as they were in Britain. His thoughts were highly original for his time. He defied conventional wisdom and criticized long-standing practices. He called attention to markets and how they worked, and he prescribed what he thought ought to be done for Britain to increase its national wealth, or "opulence."

There were others writing about these topics when Adam Smith did—the Enlightenment was filled with busy pens—but only Smith, who freely borrowed ideas from wherever he found them, is likely to be remembered today. The influential policy-makers of his day read *The Wealth of Nations* and it became a bestseller. It was admired in England as a distinguished work of Enlightenment scholarship, but was not thought by the ruling classes to be very practical. Many of his English readers thought the book was radical, even dangerous, because it advocated abolishing the special privileges and subsidies that benefited those well placed in British society. After his death, in 1790, some critics associated his ideas with those of the French Revolution, which was hardly popular within the British government and nobility; the government pursued few of his policy recommendations or changes until many years after his death.

But where Adam Smith *was* listened to was in America, the fledging country across the sea that had just recently broken away from Britain's rule. Smith never visited America, but his writings were read by many of the country's founding fathers, including Washington, Franklin, Adams, Jefferson, Hamilton, Madison, and Jay. Though these men were familiar with Smith's theories, he was not given many citations in their own writings for the reason that his observations were seen to apply to Britain, not to the United States, and Britain was a very different place. Hamilton, for example, argued extensively for why he did *not* want to adopt some of Smith's ideas, those that may have been right for Britain but not, he thought, for the United States. However, many of Adam Smith's ideas *were* right for America, if not right for Europe, and they were adopted and implemented. These contained important insights into markets, the organization of labor, the role of self-interest and the taking of risks, as well as observations on foreign trade, banking and finance, national defense, and the place of government in the economy.

The early design for an American economic structure was much shaped by debate between Hamilton and Jefferson, two stalwart political opponents. But Adam Smith might just as well have prepared it. His writings and economic ideas were there at the creation of the new republic. They were part of the crucial admixture that enabled the country to fortify its confidence in its new social and economic principles and to overcome the hazards of its early years.

Adam Smith saw the discovery of America as one of the most important events in the history of the world, and he had considerable interest in the country's ultimate development. He believed it had enormous potential, and he wrote extensively about British policies in America. He died, however, before being able to see how things turned out. But fortunately, we Americans have survived to appreciate how and where his influence has been applied in the early development of the country's economy.

In the twenty years that ended in 2000, more wealth was created in America than at any other time or place in the history of the world. Household net worth was $37 trillion, up from about $8 trillion when Ronald Reagan became President. There were then more than five million millionaires in the country. All this occurred despite a market crash in 1987, several other significant market reversals, and a recession. I wrote a book about these exciting times, called *The Wealth Creators*, which attempted to tell the story behind the boom—explaining what was going on in America to make such a boom possible and who some of the principal beneficiaries were.

My book addressed the question of "Why now?" that the boom posed, but it did not address an equally interesting question: "Why us?" Why did this happen in America more than in other places?

Perhaps the answer to that question seems self-evident. America has been and remains the world's true beacon of market capitalism, and no other large country has entrusted its future to this system to quite the same extent. But why is that? Why is America so firmly committed to private enterprise and so little interested in state-owned businesses or large-government, economic-assistance programs? How did this come about?

These questions led me onto a path of inquiry that went back to the beginnings of the country and the unique history of American enterprise. It turns out that we have always been committed to a democratic free-market system and have striven to provide space for the great American "entrepreneurial spirit" to range as far as it could.

I am grateful to my editor, Truman Talley, for his encouragement in writing this book and for his many suggestions that have improved it.

Roy C. Smith (no relation)
New York City, 2002

CHAPTER 1

ENLIGHTENMENT AND THE NEW ECONOMICS

In 1718, a twenty-four-year-old Frenchman named François Marie Arouet was released from the Bastille, where he had been imprisoned for a year because of satirical remarks critical of the French monarchy and its harsh system of social justice. The fact that someone else, not Arouet, had written the offending words did not matter much, since Arouet, though from a good family and well-introduced into society, was known as a stinging critic who could reliably be counted on to ridicule or satirize French society and its high officials. After the Bastille, he began to publish plays and sharp-tongued works of social criticism under the pen name "Voltaire." A few years later, in trouble again, he talked his prosecutors into permitting him to go

1

into exile in England instead of returning to prison. As Voltaire, he then lived much of his life outside France, and his wit, insight, and penetrating critiques influenced many throughout Europe to question their society and their assumptions about it.

At his death, in 1778, Voltaire was known as the leading literary figure of his time. His works covered wide-ranging fields, topics, and problems. They were generally held to be brilliant and influential, though almost always his viewpoints were critical, cynical, and cutting. He believed in the powers of reason and the ability of the human mind to better understand the world and to deduce explanations and solutions to problems common to all. His ideas were controversial, and often they challenged the authority of authoritarian states. His great popularity was a protection to him, but he was frequently in trouble for his criticism of conventional wisdom and those in power.

The life of Voltaire became synonymous with the period—beginning in the early eighteenth century and lasting for a hundred years or so—that is known as "The Enlightenment." This was an extraordinary time of intellectual awakening and discovery, leading to a reexamination of all that was then known about man's role in civilized society. Since the movement had evolved from the scholarly debates surrounding the Protestant Reformation, it focused on religion and philosophy, but it soon spread beyond those precincts to the natural sciences. By the mid 1700s, the intellectual capital and curiosity needed to investigate and question previous conceptions about life had been assembled. Much of what was known about the world at that time—most of which had been rigidly handed down since the darker days of the Middle Ages—came under the new light of inquiry, and many long-held assumptions, after the usual amount of resistance to the destabilizing effect of new ideas, were forever afterward seen differently.

Although Voltaire was devoted principally to philosophy and religion, the Enlightenment released throughout Europe a torrent of intellectual activity in at least three other areas: science and medicine, geography and exploration, and politics and economics. There was an effort to apply methodology and specialization to mathematics, physics, navigation, chemistry, astronomy, geography, botany, zoology, psychology, anatomy and physiology, and the understanding of disease. The efforts resulted in a pace of discovery never before experienced. In philosophy and religion, where Voltaire had a lot of company, "unauthorized" (that is, by the church) investigations into theology in its broadest sense took place. Christian moral and ethical beliefs were examined closely. So were agnosticism, pantheism, and atheism. The ancient strictures, practices, and entitlements of the Christian church and its beliefs were attacked. And there were inquiries into human rights, justice, social order, law, education, and the causes and effects of economic activity. There were no sacred cows. Much of this sudden intellectual energy was also reflected onto the arts, music, and literature. The novel was born, and the theater reborn. Handel and Bach held sway, and Hogarth, a popular satirical engraver, depicted London scenes of daily life in all its sordid detail.

Most of the intellectual activity of this time was the product of talented amateurs who painstakingly learned methodology and specialization. Intellectual recognition was open to anyone bright enough to prepare an interesting piece about a new discovery and get it published. Benjamin Franklin, a Philadelphia printer of limited education, became a respected name in Europe by presenting his discoveries in electricity to the Royal Society in 1749. Further, the borders between scientific disciplines were not well defined, and scholars, academics, and curious amateurs seemed comfortable in shifting between subjects. Franklin made important discoveries in oceanography and physiology in addition to electrical science, and invented the iron stove, bifocals, and the lightning rod, among other useful things. He was also a best-selling author of homespun philosophy. Franklin's friend, the Scottish philosopher David Hume, was, in addition, a poet, a historian and a theologian. Such polymaths were not at all uncommon in learned circles.

Fresh ideas were what counted in the Enlightenment, not

one's formal, i.e., old-fashioned, training. Anyone with a theory and a persuasive tongue could be listened to. Certainly a lot of nonsense was published and faddishly admired for a while, but there was a continuous supply of new material and more recent and accurate discoveries. Though the educated public was not large in the eighteenth century, it included the nobility (most of them landowners), government officials and rising politicians, the professional classes, intellectuals, and critics. This group of educated people could and did affect public attitudes and policies. Learned individuals bought a lot of books and kept up with what was going on in various fields. Franklin knew several of the leading European Enlightenment figures, including Voltaire and Hume. He and John Adams and Thomas Jefferson, who had also lived in London and Paris, had standing orders at booksellers in those cities for the latest works on government and economics.

One of the most far-reaching influences of the Enlightenment led to the American and French revolutions, each occurring as an expression of the fundamental "rights" of the people. Before the Enlightenment, people knew very little about rights; indeed, they didn't know they had any. Political power and all governing authority were vested in the ruler, and the people had to adapt and obey or suffer the consequences. The common citizen knew only that the system that controlled his daily social and economic life often seemed unsatisfactory, unfair, and after a certain point, intolerable. Beyond this, the American and French revolutions had little in common. The American event was really an act of secession, led by the indigenous wealthy and professional classes in response to the oppressive actions of their sovereign; the French Revolution, in which the mob overthrew and murdered its rulers, was different. But in both cases, economic issues, especially taxation unfairly applied and the allocation of wealth, rank, and privileges to favorites of the king, were among the basic causes of the popular discontent.

The European model for the political economy of the eighteenth century was essentially feudal. The king reigned supreme and could allocate properties and economic rights however he chose, as long as he maintained the power to enforce his actions and put down dissenters. The king relied upon a cohort of noblemen and officials to enforce his rules, and accordingly, he shared some of the land, largesse, and glory with them. The noblemen attempted to keep the system intact by extracting as much from those beneath them as they could short of causing insurrection and mutiny. These conditions had existed for a long time, and people had become accustomed to them and knew their "place," a measure of submission encouraged by the organized church.

What every learned person at the time knew of history

was that all previous efforts to establish any other system—either through republics or independent city-states—had fallen inevitably to tyranny, revolt, or conquest, usually at great cost to the common people. The trouble was that kings and their governments were rarely good at governing. They got into countless scrapes with neighbors and waged expensive wars to resolve them. There were also expensive royal building projects (like Versailles) to be paid for that helped drain treasuries dry. And when the coffers dried up, they had to be replenished by applying pressure in the usual place—increased taxes levied on ordinary people.

These were the realities of European economic life when Adam Smith, son of a minor public official, was born in a small village near Edinburgh in 1723. By the end of his life, in 1790, both the American and French revolutions had occurred, and another revolution—a powerful industrial one—had begun. These events changed economic life in Britain, France, and elsewhere in Europe, but the changes were forced by events—they were not planned—and all of them took place after the Enlightenment began.

Adam Smith was not the first person to write about economics, but he was the first to provide a comprehensive picture of a national economic system and how it operated. And (more important to his reputation) he was also the first to present his economic ideas at a time when practical men of affairs would be most likely to read them. His major work, *An Inquiry into the Nature and Causes of The Wealth of Nations,* was first published in the important year of 1776 and enjoyed five editions, the last appearing in 1789, the year of the French Revolution. The book explored many aspects of how people and countries earned their livelihood. In essence, it described the British economic system and ways in which it might be changed for the better, i.e., to make the country even wealthier. Thus, after a time, he came to be known as the father of modern political economics and the first of the four "classical" economists to form the profession that later emerged. The others were Thomas Malthus, who published *Essays on Population* in 1798; David Ricardo, author of *Principles of Political Economy and Taxation* (1817); and John Stuart Mill, author of *Principles of Political Economy* (1848), which first addressed the distribution of wealth.

The Wealth of Nations was widely read in Smith's own time, not only by scholarly colleagues, but also by the rich landowners of England and Scotland, who had great vested interests in the subject of wealth, and by many parliamentarians and rising, ambitious politicians. A lot of what Smith had to say was critical and probably radical, but it was presented in a way that made it acceptable to patriotic Englishmen of his time. Smith's goal was to describe why the British economic system had been so successful relative to other European nations, and how Britain's wealth and power could be further increased.

At the first treatise of its kind, and widely available, *The Wealth of Nations* was also read and discussed by those in America seeking to form a new government based on preserving "life, liberty, and the pursuit of happiness," and an economic system that could assure America of prosperity and self-sufficiency. The founders of the American republic were about to do something never done before, that is, to create a political and economic system that could operate successfully without placing all of its powers into the hands of a single governing ruler. The stakes were high for these founders, who had pledged their "lives, fortunes and their sacred honor" to the cause. They knew, intuitively perhaps, that establishing the ability of a new society to create significant wealth, both public and private, would be the ultimate test of their efforts. Without prosperity and opportunity, the society would likely give up the experiment and call back the king, or use the leverage of democracy to shake itself apart as the French did, thus ending its republican dream.

The American founding fathers, therefore, were more than eager to learn what they could about the new field of political economics. And because the country that seemed to have the most successful economy, despite its many faults, was Great Britain, Adam Smith's great work on the subject of the British economy appeared just when the Americans were most receptive to it.

WHO WAS ADAM SMITH?

Adam Smith was a reclusive, colorless Scottish academic who came to be well known for one great book, but for little else. He was born in Kirkcaldy, a town of twenty-three-hundred inhabitants, located just across the Firth of Forth from Edinburgh, where his father was the local customs collector and clerk. Less than a generation earlier, a much bullied-and-bloodied Scotland had agreed to union with Britain (in 1707), and most of its two million inhabitants were still looking for the benefits, if any.

Smith's father died just before his son's birth, so young Adam was raised solely by his mother, whose only child he was. She was a member of the landed family of Douglas, and he was well looked after as a child, though he attended the local schools, which later he declared to have been very good. He left home at fourteen (about the age of most students entering college then) to attend the University of Glasgow on a scholarship. He remained for three years, studying mathematics and natural sciences under strict but dedicated instructors. One of these was Francis Hutcheson, a humanist professor of moral philosophy and an influential mentor not only to Adam Smith, but also to many budding Scottish intellectuals of the time. In 1740, Smith received a coveted scholarship to Balliol College, Oxford, a great opportunity. The future of Scotsmen in the newly united Britain depended upon their ability to demonstrate intellectual acumen and to assimilate with the English. Both of these attributes were available at Oxford, but Smith didn't like the place, or perhaps it didn't like him. He claimed to have gained little at Oxford, where he believed that "the greater part of the public professors have . . . given up altogether even the pretense of teaching."[1] However, it is also possible that the attention given at Oxford to politics (including Scottish politics), religious dissent, and public licentiousness made him uncomfortable.

Still, after six years he completed his scholarship and returned to Scotland. Two years later, he appeared as a twenty-five-year-old public lecturer in rhetoric in Edinburgh. This was something of an entrepreneurial venture—he advertised his courses publicly and people paid to come to them—as he was not associated with the University of Edinburgh. Even so, he lectured on natural jurisprudence and politics and began to form a theme central to all his subsequent work. He advanced the theory that:

Little else is requisite to carry a state to the highest degree of opulence from the lowest barbarism but peace, easy taxes, and a tolerable administration of

11

justice; all the rest being brought by the natural course of things. All governments which thwart this natural course, which force things into another channel, or which endeavor to arrest the progress of society at a particular point, are unnatural, and to support themselves are obliged to be oppressive and tyrannical.[2]

These lectures, reflecting some of the sentiments picked up from the lectures of his mentor Francis Hutcheson, helped to make his reputation. In 1751, still in his twenties, Smith was appointed to the faculty of the University of Glasgow, first to the Chair of Logic; then soon afterward, on the unexpected death of Professor Hutcheson, he assumed the chair of Moral Philosophy. He threw himself into academic life, which, though demanding, seemed to suit him well. He taught a large "public" class every weekday morning from 7:30 to 8:30, and met this class again at noon to examine it on what he had lectured earlier. Also, from 11:00 A.M. until noon, three days a week, he lectured to a smaller, more advanced "private" class. (Even the most junior American academic today rarely teaches more than eight hours a week.) Moral philosophy was a wide-open subject at the time, and Smith used it to discuss his ideas about the formation of language, jurisprudence, and "natural" laws (i.e., forms of human rights).

In 1759, he published his first major work, *Theory of*

Moral Sentiments, in which some of his favorite themes first made their appearance. Among these were the "invisible hand," the motivational power of ambition and self-interest in determining economic outcomes, and the importance of a fair system of justice in order to preserve social order, a condition necessary to optimize opulence. (For "opulence," a word common to Smith's writings, one should substitute "national wealth" to make the meaning clearer.) These ideas became building blocks for his theory of the British economy that later appeared in *The Wealth of Nations.*

The first of these building blocks has to do with the unpredictable nature of markets. To begin with, Smith argued, human society is, in "a certain abstract philosophical light, like an immense machine, whose regular and harmonious movements produce a thousand agreeable effects." To him, a great range of social activity was captured by these machinelike characteristics, in that men pursuing their own objectives in interaction with others seemed frequently to experience outcomes that they did not foresee or expect (but that were nevertheless good for the system as a whole). What we might refer to as a doctrine of unintended consequences, Smith thought of as an "invisible hand," as in the statement, "Man is led [as if] by an invisible hand to promote an end that was no part of his intention."[3]

Many people today believe that Adam Smith's invisible hand was the essential defense for laissez-faire economic policies, i.e., those that would steer the economy to a most favorable outcome if only the government would get out of the way and let the markets do their work. It may be convenient to think this, but it is not quite what Smith had in mind. (Nor did he ever use the phrase laissez-faire—the creation of some contemporary French economists—to describe his thinking.) No doubt what Smith did mean was that human intercourse was so extensive and continuous that it established a natural marketplace in which valuable interactions were the result of unpredictable supply and demand. An investor might be motivated to jump in and become active in one area of business, only to find out later that market conditions had changed, and instead, he found himself doing something different, which may or may not produce a better effect.

One of the great conservative economists of the twentieth century, the Austrian Friedrich von Hayek, saw Adam Smith as the discoverer of "spontaneous order" (the way social institutions come to life without anyone planning for them), and another, Milton Friedman, one of laissez-faire's most dedicated supporters, has noted that there was much in Smith's work that was still important two hundred years after it was published.[4]

Adam Smith's views on ambition and self-interest as expressed in *Moral Sentiments* were also unusual for his times, when greed (avarice) was a sin and people were supposed to know their place in society and accept it. Ambition and avarice (kept within the bounds of prudence and the law) are not only laudable, Smith said, they are also beneficial for society. If people believed they could get ahead by their own efforts, then they would, in their own self-interest, endeavor to do so. If enough people did this, Smith the economist wrote, markets that followed the principles of maximizing value through incentives would emerge. But Smith the humanist noted that beyond basic needs, the *real* motivations for self-interest were vanity and the desire to show one's self off to good effect:

For what purpose is all the toil and bustle of this world? What is the end of avarice and ambition, of the pursuit of wealth, or power and preeminence? . . . From whence arises that emulation that runs through all the different ranks of men, and what are the advantages [to that] great purpose of human life which we call bettering our condition? To be observed, to be attended to, to be taken notice of with sympathy and approbation. . . . It is the vanity, not the ease or the pleasure, which interests us.[5]

Beyond self-interest, Smith believed that for any economic system to work its best (in producing opulence), it must also be based on a system of justice that is considered to be fair and effective. It is the "main pillar that upholds the whole edifice," he said, adding . . .

". . . as the violation of justice is what men will never submit to from one another, the public magistrate is under a necessity of [judiciously] employing the power of the [state] to enforce the laws. Otherwise, civil society would become a scene of bloodshed and disorder, every man revenging himself at his own hand whenever he fancied he was injured."[6]

These words became prophetic as the British government's struggles with its American colonies, already strained, grew contentious. But they also echoed the English history of longstanding struggles between landlords and tenants in Ireland and Scotland, of which Adam Smith was surely well aware.

The *Theory of Moral Sentiments* was a big success. It had six editions, made Adam Smith's name as a scholar, and propelled him into an orbit with other influential figures of the Enlightenment. In it, Smith joined a fairly small, elite group of British intellectuals focusing on social and political issues. The best-known of these were John Locke and David Hume, the latter a fellow Scot and Smith's close friend. He was also a contemporary in Britain of John Wesley (the founder of the Methodist movement), historians Thomas Carlyle and Edward Gibbon, and those wandering, critical men of letters, Dr. Samuel Johnson and James Boswell.

In 1760, now well known in philosophical circles, Smith

next turned to a series of lectures on jurisprudence at the University of Glasgow, in which he developed ideas about the origins of government, the importance of economics in social and political development, and the role of government in economic life. He started with a big-picture review of the emergence of the modern social economic system that followed the collapse of the western Roman Empire. Some sort of government would have been necessary to hold the society together, he reasoned, and to develop it in competition with other, perhaps more aggressive, predatory societies. He gave much thought to the authority of a governor to govern (he favored older, wealthier people, whom he felt the governed could more readily respect), and divided the evolution of society into four stages. These were the stages of hunters (Indians in North America), nomadic herders (Arabs), agricultural cultivators (Britain and most of Europe), and finally, the attainment of a commercial stage of trading and the use of markets, which had not really emerged by 1760. Smith believed that Britain would be the first country to reach this stage because it alone had escaped political absolutism (thanks to the Magna Carta and Oliver Cromwell) and had a long history of markets and exchanges motivated by merchants seeking to maximize their self-interests.

In forming his views, Smith drew extensively on generalizations from classical times (Greek and Roman) and on precedents from British history reaching back to

Elizabeth I and earlier. The fourth stage was a goal, still in progress. When and as it was achieved, societies could realize major increases in opulence that would protect them from enemies and give them power to extend their influence elsewhere.

Most of his *Lectures on Jurisprudence* was spent on trying to deduce how this fourth stage would work and how it could be attained. More particularly, he considered the notion of markets; the division of labor between agriculture, manufacturing, and commerce; and prices, wages, and "natural" laws that should apply to them. He also studied the role of money as a medium of exchange for goods and services, and the advantages of free trade. This was a lot of economics for a treatise on jurisprudence. These lectures contained many early sketches of ideas and opinions that appeared later in *The Wealth of Nations.*

Then, in a surprise to his biographers, Adam Smith, in his early forties, left academic life to venture out into the world. He was approached by Charles Townshend, the stepfather of a teenage Scottish duke who needed to make a grand tour of Europe. Townshend, a prominent Tory politician, was a member of the cabinet as chancellor of the exchequer from 1766–1768 and author of the so-called "Townshend Acts," which played a major part in the early days of the American Revolution.

Townshend had read *Moral Sentiments* and thought Smith would be a good influence on his stepson. Would

Smith accompany the duke as his tutor? The patronage and the money were right, so Smith would. The assignment lasted for three years (1764–1767) and was spent living in Paris for two years. There Smith met many of the leading intellectuals in the city, including Rousseau (but not Voltaire), and became familiar with much of the work in economics being done by a variety of amateur scholars, including Charles-Louis de Secondat (Baron de Montesquieu) and a group organized by François Quesnay that called themselves *Physiocrats*. This group coined the phrase laissez-faire, which meant a sort of utopian natural economic order that if left alone (i.e., unregulated), would develop into an optimally effective free-market system. Otherwise, however, Adam Smith, still a dry, morally correct, abstemious Scottish bachelor, seemed not to have been much impressed by France and its many attractions. After returning to Britain, he never left the country again and spent the next ten years, mainly isolated in Kirkcaldy, working on *The Wealth of Nations*.

Though a practical man who could tolerate the need for national interests to sometimes supersede his economic principles, Smith's *The Wealth of Nations* was really quite radical, and in that sense, impractical. Though readable today, it is long, sometimes tedious, filled with long-out-of-date references (some of which, economist Charles Kindleberger notes were out of date even in 1776[7]) and much of it arguing now long-settled economic policy disputes. In parts, it is witty, scathing, and whimsical. Smith certainly did not hesitate to say what he thought, and a lot of what he thought was extreme at the time. Many works by the great Enlightenment figures were thought to be radical; they challenged conventional wisdom head-on and questioned policies and actions that had been bedrock orthodoxy for generations. Today, these ideas do not seem radical at all.

The basis for many of Smith's theories was no more than deductive reasoning, not derived from statistical data or other evidence. You either found the reasoning logical and thus hard to refute, or you didn't. Those of Smith's readers who were convinced could warmly accept his ideas, which were scholarly, temperate in language, and persuasive. Those who were not convinced, however, had little grounds on which to take offense. Smith, after all, was a bookish scholar, not a dangerous troublemaker. And no one could quarrel with his patriotic objective, which was to delineate policies that would increase the wealth of Great Britain and enable the nation to draw ahead of its rivals. So, if you found his ideas leading directly to reforms that would threaten your personal wealth and control of it, you might call less attention to his notions by simply suggesting that they were impractical. This, of course, is what most of the landed gentry did do.

The genius of *The Wealth of Nations* was in its extreme simplicity, and its success was facilitated by the work of previous writers who paved the way for its reception, argued Cambridge Professor W. Cunningham in a comprehensive history of English commerce and industry published in 1892. Smith had rivals in Britain, chiefly Joseph Massie and Sir James Steuart, and several in France, including Montesquieu, Condorcet and the *philosophes*. Massie and Steuart both addressed British mercantilism, but neither suggested any change in the system. Mercantilism had been used by the British since the earliest days of their overseas colonies to ensure, through a series of economic policies, that the colonies would remain dependent upon, and exploitable by, the mother country. Massie wanted more information before suggesting anything concrete. Steuart was mainly an advocate for a central system (such as mercantilism) that could be carried out as national policy. Smith was sufficiently influenced by Montesquieu to attempt to capture his "spirit of the people" for his own system, but he did not know how to go beyond the abstraction. He accepted Condorcet's ideas of addressing economic issues with humanistic considerations in mind, but he dismissed the arguments of the other French economists on technical grounds.

The simplicity derived from Smith's basic claims that any government-controlled system of commerce was an impediment to the working of the market, and he said therefore that the British system in 1776 was indeed seriously flawed. He was able to reduce all economic considerations into a novel and comprehensive theory of the marketplace, and he expanded his notion of the marketplace to embrace international trade. According to his theory, wealth would result from the production of items that could be sold in markets for money (gold and silver), a commodity like other raw materials. If left alone, free of monopolies and various forms of interference by government-appointed agents, markets would be able to allocate resources optimally, and labor, motivated by wealth-maximizing self-interest and division into efficient specialization, would respond accordingly. Then the marketplace would expand and attract competition and lower prices. The flow of goods and money to pay for them would determine prices and exchange rates, which naturally must adjust to imbalances. Trade, therefore, would benefit all participants, a concept that economists widely believe to be true today, but that consensus was achieved only recently. But if trade was to increase, Smith argued, it must be free—let loose from the shackles of protectionism, the heaviest of which was the time-honored mercantile system.

The book that assured Smith's place in history thus contained much of his earlier work interspersed with the timely events that were increasingly of interest to the audience he wanted most to reach—the influential ranks who made the rules in England. The most important event then drawing the attention of Britain's most influential people was the development in North America of a strong resistance to British rule and influence. This was a matter of great concern to the British, and considerable debate both favoring and opposing the American position developed in Parliament and outside it. It was the preeminent political-economic issue of the day, and Adam Smith felt he had to address it in his book.

The underlying economic system responsible for the American problems was broken and needed to be fixed, many people in government and business argued before 1776. Smith agreed, and he discussed a number of the colonial issues in his book, starting with the idea that the Seven Years' War (1755–1763, called the French and Indian War in America) had greatly increased Britain's national debt and the Americans ought to be expected to help pay it down. The British defense of America, Smith said, "led to the liberty, security and property which they have since enjoyed." Thus the Americans could be taxed, he concluded, but added that the taxes should be accompanied by freedom of trade between all parts of the Empire and the admission of the North American colonies into a form of union with Britain, such as Scotland had experienced in 1707. Union would entail representation in Parliament on the basis of the amount of taxes paid as a proportion of the total taxes levied upon Great Britain.

These were powerful ideas—ones also proposed by others but not seriously considered during the American crisis—and to understand them better, a review of how the British economic system worked in 1776 will be helpful.

THE BRITISH ECONOMIC SYSTEM

In 1884, the historian Arnold Toynbee gave a series of lectures at Oxford on the Industrial Revolution in England. The course was divided into three parts, the first of which was devoted to "Adam Smith and the England of his Time." This set of lectures included a picture of the economic system about which Smith was writing, the methods of regulation and protection of industry as they existed in 1760, and an outline and review of *The Wealth of Nations*. Reading these lectures today is as good as taking Toynbee's course. They are dynamic, interesting, and filled with provocative personal commentary and opinion. They start with some basic information. Britain's economy had never really been studied before Smith, and data were scarce, but it was clear that in 1760, not much was different from earlier times. The country had about 8.5 million people, most of them rural and engaged in agriculture. London was the largest city, holding about one-sixth of the population.

Agriculture was becoming more efficient, and food production was better, but Toynbee did not see much evidence yet of the "agricultural revolution" that preceded and enabled the Industrial Revolution. The improvements in agriculture meant that more people could or would have to move to towns and provide the labor supply for the factories. But it also meant that because of the improvements, food production was greater and prices lower, so people had more to eat, were healthier, and had more time and energy to spend on activities other than just staying alive.

Toynbee also noted that well before the Industrial Revolution, manufactures (especially those related to the woolen textiles business) were already an important part of the economy, with exports in 1770 accounting for as much as £4 million worth about $480 million today), or between a third and a fourth of all exports. The weaving of woolen cloth had been an important sector of the economy since the 1300s, when the necessary skills were imported from Flanders. Increasing demand for wool led to large enclosures of land (for sheep to graze) and the forced expulsion from it of tenant farmers, who made up a large part of the English and Scottish populations that emigrated to Ireland and North America.

After wool, the iron trade was next in importance, though it was considered in Adam Smith's time to be a decaying industry. In 1760, English furnaces produced about twenty thousand tons annually and imported about the same amount. The chief demand for iron was for weapons and armaments, though the hardware trades were starting to flourish. The cotton and linen trades, which would be the principal British industries to benefit from the Industrial Revolution, were just beginning. Some, but only a few, of the important new inventions had come on line.

There was enough manufacturing, however, for Adam Smith to develop one of his main themes in *The Wealth of Nations,* that of the increased efficiency that comes from the division of labor into specialities. Most factory workers then were agricultural laborers employed part-time. Workers ought to be one or the other, Smith said—either farmers or factory men. If so, they would not waste time getting to and from their respective places of work, or have to make themselves available for one or the other work at conflicting times. And they could learn specialized tasks that with repetition they could do efficiently as they moved up the learning curve. Smith illustrates this with a charming report of his observations of a factory that specialized in making pins.

Still, according to Toynbee, the market for finished manufactures was rather small because of the many problems with transportation, labor, and finance. Roads were "execrable," unsafe, and deadly slow, though the first canal appeared in England in 1755. There were many local restrictions on employment and labor mobility, especially through laws related to apprenticeships. Municipal governments could set wages, and they maintained laws that forbade laborers from combining for the purpose of negotiating wages. Finance, too, was very undeveloped. The

Bank of England existed, but before 1759, it did not issue any banknotes of less than £20 (about $2,500 today). As late as 1750, there were no more than twelve "bankers' shops" in all of London. The capital-intensive portion of the Industrial Revolution clearly began later. But, for all these economic obstacles, British exports were increasing, having doubled since 1700. The colonies were the chief markets, accounting for a third of all exports. Toynbee noted that in 1770, America took three-quarters of all the manufactures of Manchester (wool and cotton) and that exports to Jamaica were nearly as great as they had been to all British plantations in 1704. The shipping trade had, accordingly, also doubled during the century.[8]

The British have been subjects of a monarch since the nation's earliest days. Much of the law and many precedents for governing British society were handed down from the feudal system of the Middle Ages, some of them going back before the Norman Conquest in 1066. The British monarch (like those of the rest of Europe) ruled by the divine right of God, and in the beginning, he was all-powerful and not to be challenged. Of course there were contests to see who became monarch, but otherwise, the reigning king or queen was the repository of all economic power. The British Crown, however, required the consent of Parliament to impose taxes, and Parliament did not always go along. Money was needed for wars, for building, and to maintain the splendid appearance of the monarch.

The king owned vast amounts of land, from which rents were due him, and had the power to seize land or property belonging to others. The nobility (mainly landowners) was dependent on the king for land, titles, and other favors, and the king was not above finding ways for the nobility to repay the Crown for the largesse. The nobility also had a lot to do with designating who ran for seats in Parliament. Played skillfully, the king's hand held all the necessary cards to make the system work indefinitely.

Occasionally, money would run short and extraordinary measures would be presented to Parliament, or taken unilaterally by the king (borrowing, for example), but the system, as poorly refined or controlled as it was, worked for long periods of time. Queen Elizabeth I, who reigned for forty-five years during the sixteenth century, was intent upon expanding Britain's ability to generate wealth and frugal with her expenses. She established British preeminence at sea and used it to harass the Spanish and to explore the world. Sea power led to colonizing India and the West Indies and, ultimately, North America.

Elizabeth was succeeded by a series of less wise or adept monarchs (the Stuarts), who earned less for the treasury and spent more from it. Charles I was the last British king to insist on absolute power, and he provoked Parliament into the Civil Wars of 1642–1649, and his own overthrow and execution by the Commonwealth government of Oliver Cromwell. In 1658, Cromwell died and the monarchy was restored. Charles II came to the throne only after agreeing to share power with Parliament, and (largely because of this concession) the British monarchy has survived since, unlike the other monarchies of Europe that remained absolutist.

Britain, however, by the restoration of Charles II, had become a "constitutional" monarchy (though the British constitution is not a written document per se; it is based on precedent and time-honored ways), and its economic management had to meet certain minimal tests of sensibility to pass the scrutiny of its elected Parliament. After Charles II was succeeded by his incompetent and controversial brother James II, events led rapidly downhill to the "Glorious Revolution of 1688," after which James II was expelled, Protestantism was restored, and William of Orange and his wife Mary Stuart became co-monarchs. After Queen Mary's death (the last of the Stuarts), Parliament consented to offer the Crown to the son of a great-grandson of James I, the son of the Second Elector of Hanover, who, at fifty-four, became George I of Great Britain in 1714. George never understood the English language or the workings of Parliament very well, and took long vacations in Hanover, so the British got what they wanted: a legitimate, unambitious king who could be ruled by Parliament. George I died in 1727, passing the Crown to a son he disliked but who shared many of his personal characteristics. George II was more kingly and learned

English, but he abided by the limits on his power and income placed on them by Parliament. He left governing to his cabinet, headed by an able prime minister, Robert Walpole, who for twenty years was able to preserve the peace and increase British prosperity.

The king retained the power to make important appointments, but the power of the cabinet and the bureaucracy to distribute contracts, charters, and many other favors grew under the new political spoils system devised by Walpole, a man widely considered to be completely amoral. "Influence" (on the designation of contracts and appointments) was bought and sold. No man was more, or less, than the grand total of the influence he could bring to bear before Walpole and his cohorts. Merit had little to do with most issues. The trading of influence, however, dominated the *realpolitik* of the day, and almost nothing mattered more. Bribery, payoffs, skimming, and other forms of external payments were common, as was a continuous effort by incumbents to secure appointments for members of their families and friends.

These practices placed a heavy drag on the economic system, which accordingly, often produced inferior results. It was not a system designed to maximize output, but instead, one intended to protect and preserve social positions and the economic status quo. It was a poor system for increasing the prosperity of the country as a whole, but it actually achieved that to a greater degree than did most of the rest of Europe, where systems based on absolute powers of monarchies were even less market oriented or efficiency minded.

Trade was the growth industry of the eighteenth century. The discovery of precious metals, sugar, and tobacco in the New World, and spices, coffee, and tea in the East Indies, changed the world. Locating these goods and importing them to Europe, as well as organizing the African slave trade to develop plantations in America, offered the potential for huge profits. Nations that secured such overseas resources were assured of national wealth and strategic value for years to come. As a result, the major nations scrambled for colonies in fierce competition with one another. It was nations that competed then, not companies, and governments supplied the means of competition: the merchant ships and crews, the ports and infrastructure to support trading, and the navies to protect them. Monarchs invested in voyages of discovery, but called upon wealthy merchants to acquire charters to develop particular areas, for which the merchants would provide the capital necessary for ships and settlement in exchange for some of the profits, the Crown retaining the rest.

Joint stock companies (such as the South Sea Company, the East India Company, and the Virginia Company) raised capital through the world's first "privatization" issues by selling stock to wealthy speculators on the London Exchange. The Crown and many government officials

31

invested in these deals, and it was generally expected that in one way or another, the government would assure the success of the ventures. It was difficult to tell where the interests of the company ended and those of the state began. Weighted down by patronage, inefficiency, and corruption, these early experiments in monopolies often produced very unsatisfactory results (described in *The Wealth of Nations*) for both investors and taxpayers. But in a world of limited commercial development, in which neither investment vehicles nor skilled corporate operators existed or competed with one another, this system was probably as good as it could be. The increase in the wealth and colonial possessions of Britain after 1700, especially relative to Spain, France, Holland, and Portugal, was no doubt a direct result of this effort to utilize private capital under royal charters to develop colonial properties.

One consequence of the scramble for trade was that the prosperity of one country was thought to be incompatible with that of another. "If one country profited by trade, it seemed to do so at the expense of its neighbors," noted Toynbee, suggesting the idea that all trade was a zero-sum game. Winners' gains came out of the share of the losers. As one country grew in riches at the expense of another, it could capitalize on its gains by committing more to military expense, for conquest or defense, or by having more liquid funds available to dedicate to commercial activity, thus also extending national power.

In the eighteenth century, Britain and other countries developed the idea that gold and silver were the most durable parts of a nation's wealth and should be accumulated by all possible means and hoarded. They could be accumulated only if exports of goods and commodities exceeded imports, the difference being paid for by a transfer of precious metals. This idea became the economic rationale for mercantilism, and numerous policies were adopted to implement it. To be sure that precious metals remained in Britain, laws were passed that prohibited their export. Adam Smith pointed out that this caused considerable disruption to the normal working of overseas trade and investment needed to pay for goods and services abroad. Smuggling also increased to get around these rules, so the focus of government policy turned to managing the balance of exports and imports, and policies were adopted to restrict imports to necessary raw materials and to promote exports of high value-added manufactured goods or services.

These restrictions were enforced by tariffs, quotas, and prohibitions, and by legislation such as the Navigation Acts, first imposed in 1651 and amended many times. The Acts essentially required that British trade be carried in British ships, but they created a monopoly for the British merchant marine that raised shipping costs and ultimately operated against British interests in Europe, the Baltic, and some neutral ports. But the monopoly worked very well for the British in its controlled colonial areas, though these were insignificant when the Navigation Acts were first enacted.

British economic policies were openly protectionist, in keeping with the government's understanding of trade economics. They were further defended on the grounds of national defense (for Britannia to rule the seas, it had to have something for her ships to do), and the argument that the stimulus of trade would help overcome the apathy and dullness of a purely agricultural population. The problem was, however, that British exports were some other country's imports, and Britain's principal trade rivals had also figured out the balance-of-payments idea. Tariff wars broke out across Europe and nullified much of the benefits of trade altogether. The real benefits of the British mercantile system, therefore, were to be achieved by trading with primitive, weak economies that had no domestic manufacturing industries to protect and plenty of desirable raw materials for sale cheaply. China, India, and the East Indies were prime prospects, but these were also attractive to other European countries. So deals had to be made to secure colonies with exclusive trading rights. The British and the French struggled over India, Malaya, and Indochina. The British and the Dutch vied over South Africa and the Spice Islands, and China became something of a free-for-all, with everyone getting a bit of something. In the Americas, the Europeans competed with each other for colonies in the Caribbean and on the North American mainland.

By Adam Smith's time, it was apparent that of all these colonial efforts, the British had won the jackpot in North America. Its colonies there had become highly fruitful suppliers of valuable raw materials, and also important customers for Britain's increasing manufacturing output. British bottoms carried the trade, and its warships could be provisioned with American timber and manned by impressed American sailors. British banks financed and insured the trade, and British agents took commissions at both ends. Rather than be jailed at home, British criminals could be "transported" to America, a land more than large enough to absorb all the excess population of the British Isles. A small number of British-born officials governed the colonies, which for more than a hundred and fifty years were law-abiding and peaceful. The system was self-financing, added greatly to the British balance of payments and accumulation of wealth, and its size and location offered major strategic advantages to Britain in the struggle with its European rivals for power in the western hemisphere.

It was certainly a goose that laid golden eggs, and if the British treated the colonies exploitatively, that was only to be expected. Toynbee described their regard for the colonies as little more than the "farms and markets of the mother country." Most American export goods could not be sold anywhere except in Britain, though the British often resold and reshipped these goods to other countries. Foodstuffs and certain other commodities already produced by British landowners could not be exported from America at all. All imports from other countries in Europe were prohibited to America so that the British might monopolize the American market. American manufacturing was suppressed; for example, all textile and iron manufacturing was prohibited, even nail making. Unquestionably, the British rule of the American economy was stringent and greatly thwarted its potential development.

But it was the only system the colonists knew, and surely the best one to select had there been a choice between similar colonial systems run by the French, Dutch, or Spanish. Without British rule, the unprotected North American colonies would have been exposed to the threat of raids and invasions by other countries, which could have been ruinous. As it was, the colonies were prosperous, lawful, and secure. Land and food were plentiful and cheap, and life was free of many of the religious and class-ridden disadvantages of British society. But the French and Indian War precipitated challenges—economic and political—to Britain's rule of these colonies and posed a threat to the immovable wall of the mercantile system that many Britons thought was the secret to its national economic success. As Toynbee pointed out in his lectures, "Nothing contributed more than this commercial system to the Declaration of Independence."[9]

Toynbee knew that Adam Smith had come to many of the same conclusions. Smith was critical of Britain's colonial administration in America. He spent a lot of time, space, and wit in his book addressing the effect of mercantilism on the colonies and the misdirected policies of colonial administration. "A great empire has been established for the sole purpose of raising up a nation of customers who should be obliged to buy from the shops of our different producers . . . but for the sake of that little enhancement of price which this monopoly might afford producers, the home-consumers have been burdened with the whole expense of maintaining and defending that empire." Indeed, he added, maintaining the compliance of the Americans had cost hundreds of millions of pounds, and "new debts had been contracted over and above all that had been expended for the same purpose in former wars."

Even so, Smith claimed, there was much more at stake than that. Allowing America to develop into a vast nation of unquestioned economic value, which would transfer much of its trade and need for skills to Britain, would be a far wiser course. And the stupidest course of all was to try to win a commercial war by attacking Britain's own customers. If as a result of the war, Britain lost the customers, where would they go but into the arms of Britain's economic rivals? How would Britain ever recover from such a self-inflicted economic loss? Smith agreed with Burke that however much offense the Americans had given (and he conceded that they had offended considerably), and no matter how undeservedly, it could not be in Britain's interest to go to war with them.

Smith, the economist, was not much interested in the constitutional question of the day. Could America be taxed without being represented in Parliament? He thought they could be. But, he said, without offering union (i.e., representation in Parliament), they should not be. What little was gained from the proceeds of taxation would scarcely repay a fraction of the cost of acquiring it by force, or (much worse) of losing the captive American trade altogether. These were concerns that Smith and others in Britain already knew were valid when the Americans instituted boycotts of British goods (their "non-importation" campaign) after the Stamp Tax was imposed in 1765. The boycott had a huge effect on the British merchants and manufacturers engaged in the American trade, who of course carried their concerns to the government. The tax was repealed soon afterward, but ill feeling and distrust germinated on both sides.

Within a few months of its publication, Professor Cunningham said that *The Wealth of Nations* "had become a considerable power." Seemingly, it had something in it for everyone, and it appeared to gather bipartisan support in the Parliament. In 1777, Lord North borrowed some of its suggestions on taxation, and William Pitt (the elder) openly praised it. North was prime minister during the American Revolution and no friend to the colonists, and Pitt, who had been replaced by George III, had long been an opponent of the government's North American policies. In fact, Americans liked Pitt so much that they renamed Fort Duquesne, captured from the French in western Pennsylvania, Fort Pitt in his honor (it is now Pittsburgh).

All of England knew that the American issue was important and might seriously affect Britain's future. According to Smith . . .

In the course of little more than a century, perhaps the produce of America might exceed that of British taxation. The seat of the Empire would then naturally remove itself to that part of the Empire which contributed most to the general defense and support of the whole.

Thus, he was saying, once the Americas reached their peak in a century or so, the British government would earn more in America than it could collect in taxes at home, so it would "naturally" just pack up and move the British capital to someplace like Pittsburgh, to run the Empire from the seat of its economic power. The British Crown and Parliament relocating to Pittsburgh? That would be something!

THE AMERICAN QUESTION

The first successful British colony in North America was established at Jamestown, Virginia, in 1607; the first unsuccessful one was tried at Roanoke Island, North Carolina, by Sir Walter Raleigh in Elizabethan days. The Jamestown expedition was organized by businessmen who obtained a royal charter and financed it by the sale of stock in the Virginia Company. Its purpose was to make money by finding valuable minerals, crops, or other products that could be sold in Europe. The effort got off to a rocky start and was almost abandoned in 1610, but it held together until the introduction of tobacco from the Caribbean in 1613, and it finally prospered.

By 1620, when the Pilgrims were making their way to Plymouth Rock, the Jamestown colony numbered about a thousand inhabitants, including a small number of Negro slaves. In 1622, however, an Indian attack, coordinated over a large area, wiped out about a third of the colony, and the financial consequences ruined the company. In 1624, King Charles I canceled the royal charter, and Virginia became a Crown colony governed by a local legislature and headed by a governor appointed in London. Subsequently, other colonies were founded and slowly developed. Though Britain possessed several hugely profitable sugar-growing islands in the Caribbean and a budding empire in India, Africa, and Southeast Asia, the North American colonies became its most valuable overseas possession. For this reason, Adam Smith claimed that the "discovery of North America and that of a passage to the East Indies by the way of the Cape of Good Hope *are the two greatest and most important events ever recorded in the history of mankind.*" (Emphasis added.)

What made North America important to the British was, first, possessing its enormous economic potential, and, second, not having any of its major rivals, France, Spain or Holland possess it instead. After the fall of French Quebec to General Wolfe in 1759, Britain controlled all of North America from the St. Lawrence River to Florida, having banished the Dutch from New York in 1664. The Spanish, however, still controlled Florida, the Caribbean, and much of the Gulf of Mexico, including New Orleans and access to the Mississippi River.

By the time of the American Revolution, North America had become Britain's largest supplier of raw materials and its biggest market for exported manufactures. Until the middle 1750s, relations between the mother country and the colonies had been without incident. But the French and Indian War changed everything.

In 1754, without a declaration of war, hostilities broke

out between Britain and France in America. A year later, Britain had signed an alliance with Prussia, and France had made an alliance with Austria. This was history's first global conflict, and much of it was fought at sea in the Caribbean and in North America. The French, allied with various Indian tribes, repeatedly attacked British North America along its frontiers, delaying settlement and threatening to separate its northern and southern colonies by raising havoc between them. The British increased the powers of the colonies' governors and dispatched regular troops, commanded by professional officers, to address the issues and sort things out. They expected the Americans to help by contributing men and equipment to the military effort and by absorbing some of the cost of an undertaking that was essentially to protect them from the French.

The Americans did cooperate, but the British found the military problems more difficult than they expected. After the humiliating defeat of British General Edward Braddock in Ohio in 1755, the cost and involvement of the British regular army in America rose substantially. So did the efforts of the increasingly arrogant and assertive British to extract an American share, by force if necessary. Orders were issued to draft American troops and impose taxes, and these met resistance from the colonists.

It is an infringement of our basic rights as Englishmen, the colonists said, for you to impose such things on us that have not been ratified by our own legislatures. Further, we

are not governed by your Parliament, as we are not represented there. We have our own parliaments (legislatures),
and just as the British constitution prohibits the imposition
of taxes that have not been consented to by Parliament, we
believe that the only taxes we are obliged to pay are those
imposed by our legislatures, which tax us well enough
already, thank you very much!

The British brushed this argument aside (it had been
heard before from Ireland), but in the end, they found the
increasing resistance to their efforts so strong that they
agreed to a pragmatic compromise. Instead of imposing
new taxes, the British governors would request the colonial
legislatures to supply men and money as a "voluntary contribution" to the war effort. The compromise worked for
the duration of the war, but the British felt that the unruly
colonies had been ungrateful and impertinent, while the
Americans' continuous exposure to the arrogant, demanding, heavy-handed behavior of British officers and officials
greatly strained their relations. The Americans, however,
learned after Braddock's and others' defeats that the
British were not invincible in frontier skirmishes, and
indeed, that their own forces had acquitted themselves
well. The war ended in 1763, but it had increased the colonial budget tenfold, and the British costs of the war had to
be recovered.

The British government, annoyed with the uncoopera-
tive, unpatriotic conduct of the colonists and facing a tax

revolt of its own at the time, decided the best way to proceed was to impose one or more direct taxes on the
colonists as part of their share of the "Imperial" cost of the
successful war with France. The outcome of the war, after
all, had brought many benefits to North America, and if the
colonists did not like their share of the cost, too bad. They
were British subjects and had to do as they were told. To
implement this policy, the British passed the Sugar Act in
1764, which imposed a small tax on molasses imported
from the Caribbean.

Benjamin Franklin, then serving as agent in London for
both Pennsylvania and Massachusetts, was asked at the
time to negotiate with the British on behalf of the colonists.
He had a long history of negotiating with British officials,
beginning in 1754 when at a meeting with royal governors
in Albany, New York, he had proposed that the North
American colonies be united with Great Britain, as Scotland had been in 1707, and become represented in Parliament. This would bind the colonies with the mother
country against the French and Indians, Franklin argued,
and render the taxation issues moot. Franklin was ignored
then, and he was ignored again in 1765 when he offered the
British a distinction between forms of taxation: "external"
taxes, such as duties applied to trade, and "internal" taxes,
which would be assessed by the British directly to defray
non-American, British expenses. Franklin said (ten years
before the revolution) that he thought the Americans would

accept the former, but not the latter, because such were not only unconstitutional, but they were also likely to be unending—a problem for the British in India, for example, should not be relieved by taxing Americans.

Franklin's efforts were unsuccessful, and indeed, possibly counterproductive. In 1765, the Stamp Act, levied on all paper transactions and designed to raise about £60,000 per year, ($7.2 million today), met with enormous resistance in America when it was introduced. The Americans, encouraged by Franklin, responded with a boycott of British goods that reduced British-American trade by £300,000 ($36 million, or about 7 percent), the passage of the Virginia Resolves (led by an enraged Patrick Henry asking to be given "liberty or death"), and the formation in Boston of the irrepressible Sons of Liberty. The tax was repealed the following year, but Parliament asserted its "right" to tax the colonies in the future, and bitter feelings remained on both sides.

Then, in 1767, came the Quartering Act and the so-called Townshend Acts that involved import duties on everything but tea. (Adam Smith's former patron Charles Townshend, the stepfather of the duke, was chancellor of the exchequer at the time and the duties were named for him. He died later that year.) In 1768, one of John Hancock's ships (named *Liberty*) was seized for not paying custom duties and a riot ensued in Boston, requiring the British to send two regiments from Halifax. In 1770, the

Boston Massacre occurred, and in 1773, the Boston Tea Party. Tensions escalated on both sides and finally, in 1775, a year before the publication of *The Wealth of Nations,* the Battle of Lexington and Concord erupted, in which shots were fired that were "heard 'round the world." *The Wealth of Nations* was delayed at the printers, no doubt because Adam Smith was making last-minute revisions of his analysis of the British colonial policies and their inherent contradictions.

The late Barbara Tuchman offered a poignant analysis of the British loss of North America in her book *The March of Folly,* published in 1984. The British interest in preserving a benign, peaceful relationship with the colonies was widely evident, she said—

Yet for fifteen years of deteriorating relations . . . successive British ministries, in the face of constant warnings by men and events, repeatedly took measures that injured the relationship. However justifiable in principle, these measures insofar as they progressively destroyed goodwill and the voluntary connection, were demonstrably unwise in practice, besides being impossible to implement except by force. Since force could only mean enmity, the cost of the effort, even if successful, was clearly greater than the possible gain. In the end, Britain made rebels where there had been none.[10]

Tuchman goes on to quote Edmund Burke, America's Irish-born supporter in Parliament, as noting that the "retention of America was worth far more to the mother country economically, politically, and even morally than any sum that might be raised by taxation, or even any principle so-called of the Constitution." This was Adam Smith's view as well, and it was given wide circulation. Nevertheless, right in the middle of modern history's greatest time of intellectual awakening—much of it happening on England's very doorsteps—the disastrous British policies in North America were put into effect, placing far more importance on the principle of demanding respect and submission than on the other important issues that were at stake.

Ministers were largely of the nobility in Britain. Tuchman noted that the government came from "200 families (inclusive of 176 peerages) in 1760, [who] knew each other from school and university, were related through chains of cousins, in-laws, stepparents and siblings of second and third marriages, married each others' sisters, daughters and widows, and constantly exchanged mistresses . . . appointed each other to office, and secured for each other places and pensions." Of twenty-seven persons who filled high office from 1760–1780, she calculated that twenty had attended one of two boarding schools and either Oxford or Cambridge, and then gone off on a grand European tour. Further, she noted, two were dukes, two marquises, ten were earls, two were Scottish or Irish peers, six were younger sons of peers, and only five were commoners. Peers, of course, owned most of the land, controlled most of the seats in Parliament, and most of the vast quantity of patronage of the times, and had most of the money. Many peers were perfectly qualified for their duties in government, but according to Tuchman, others were not. Charles Townshend, she points out, was a son of a viscount who, according to one contemporary observer, had the capacity to be "the greatest man of his age, if his faults had only been moderate." He suffered from an "immoderate passion for fame," in addition to being "arrogant, flippant, unscrupulous, unreliable and given to reversing himself by 180 degrees when necessary."[11] He was ignorant of issues, studied them not at all, and was mainly known for a sharp, fast wit. In short, Townshend was a man who needed the system of aristocracy that had put him where he was, and he could be expected to defend it unhesitatingly when it was threatened.

For many peers, their favorite sport was found in politics and keeping track of who was in or out at court. Presiding over all this was a new king, George III, who ascended to the throne in 1760 at the age of twenty-one and promptly changed prime ministers by dismissing William Pitt, the most able statesman of his time. The search for favor and for favorites had begun anew, and George had a lot of patronage to hand out. But he was adamant about any of his colonies or dominions leaving the Empire without permission. British kings had had enough trouble from the Irish and the Scots, even just since the Hanoverians had arrived, without wanting to see more trouble in America. Powerful rulers did not let valuable territories walk away, nor did they let people of lesser rank treat them with disrespect. These simple Americans were supposed to do as they were told, the king must have thought, and if they did not, they would be taught a lesson. When such thoughts enter the head of the king, it is not a surprise if others in the nobility share it—others such as the dukes, marquises, earls, barons, and those making up the government and controlling the large English system of patronage.

After a slow start, Britain's prominent overseas possession had become the several separate colonies of North America. These had overtaken the wealthy sugar islands of the Caribbean in importance, as they had become, in aggregate, Britain's most important two-way trading partner. But after a long, uneventful relationship, during which the colonies were steadfastly loyal to the Crown, even throughout the English Civil War, relations had soured considerably. By the time Adam Smith sat down to write *The Wealth of Nations,* a few years after the successful conclusion of the French and Indian War, the colonies began openly to resist British efforts to govern them. Ultimately, this led to war, a seven-year struggle to win the independence that the Americans finally proclaimed in 1776.

After the British defeat at the battle of Saratoga in 1777, Smith was turned to for advice on the American issues. He was asked by Alexander Wedderburn, solicitor general in Lord North's administration, to provide some thoughts based on his studies of the American Question. Webberburn, a Scot and a friend, was no doubt offering Adam Smith a chance to perform before the powerful government leaders in London, and Smith took the assignment seriously.

Americans knew Wedderburn as the villain who had savaged their greatest statesman, the elderly, much-respected Benjamin Franklin, before the Privy Council in 1774 over the issue of publication in Boston of some stolen letters of Governor Thomas Hutchinson and others. This was Britain's chance to express its true views on the situation in America and those who had lived there loyally for generations. Wedderburn, however, outdid himself in invective, in calumny and insult, to roars of approval from the audience. Franklin stood silent during the attack, inwardly outraged. The incident convinced Franklin that despite his nearly sixteen years of living in England, and the acquisition of many well-placed friends, his efforts to mend colonial relations and keep them on an even keel had been wasted. The British thought little more of Americans than they did of the Irish, a people they had suppressed cruelly for centuries. After Wedderburn's attack, Franklin knew that he was an American, not a Briton, and he left the country as soon as he could to join the Continental Congress and assist it in its effort to become independent. Wedderburn's moment propelled him further into the circles whose approval he wanted (he later became Earl of Rosslyn), but he certainly failed to attend to his country's longer-term interests that day.

Adam Smith's Scottish biographers, R. H. Campbell and A. S. Skinner, note that his views on the "contest with America exerted little influence on government policy" except in one important case: Ireland was given parliamentary union with Britain in 1800, when the younger William Pitt, who was well schooled in *The Wealth of Nations*, argued that such an act would increase trade, despite a strong effort to raise the frightening specter of Catholic emancipation by Alexander Wedderburn.

THE ENLIGHTENMENT COMES TO AMERICA

It was just the sort of unbending, Old-World system that brought on the American Revolution, one rooted in traditional practices and unwilling to look beyond them that Voltaire and other European Enlightenment figures sought to overturn with their criticism. There were not many Americans other than Franklin who had given the issues much thought until the colonies began to unite in their opposition to the Townshend Acts. Indeed, most of the founding fathers were unknown at the time of the Acts, and came to be regarded as Enlightenment figures only when the Revolution was over.

Thomas Jefferson rose to fame as the author of the Declaration of Independence, and he later revealed many other talents and interests beyond politics. Jefferson was a farmer, a scientist, an architect, a social philosopher, as well as a crafty politician. Alexander Hamilton and James Madison became known for leading the debates on the American Constitution, but they also exhibited many other enlightened interests and capabilities later on. However, as their tasks focused on building a new government, many of the founders became acquainted with numerous European Enlightenment intellectuals, whose works they studied carefully. Almost fifteen years after the Declaration was published, John Adams wrote a book called *Defense of the Constitutions of Government of the United States of America,* which was published in London before he returned from that city to take up the vice-presidency, after the French Revolution had begun. He worked hard on this piece, hoping to convince the skeptical British. He laced it with references to respected contemporary European thinkers who had something useful to say about human nature and affairs; these included Voltaire, Samuel Johnson, Alexander Pope, and Adam Smith.[12] He might have also included America's political allies in England, Edmund Burke and William Pitt, or some of Franklin's scientific friends, or the *philosophes* of Paris, all of whom in some way offered original ideas or encouragement pointing toward a better system of government than the ill-administered one under which the Americans were struggling.

But whatever their achievements, even the greatest figures of the Enlightenment, perhaps even all of them taken together, were outweighed in impact and lasting importance by the contribution of a small number of obscure Americans who bravely laid down the design of a new democracy and a new economic system. John Adams, in his *Thoughts on Government* (1776), said that it was . . .

the will of heaven that we should be thrown into existence at a period when the greatest philosophers and lawgivers of antiquity would have wished to live . . . when circumstances provided an opportunity of beginning government anew from the foundation and building as they choose. How few of the human race have ever had an opportunity of choosing a system of government for themselves.[13]

CHAPTER 2

———◆◦◆———

COLONIAL ENTERPRISE

At the time of the Revolution, there were about two and a half million people in the American colonies, living in a narrow strip along an eighteen-hundred-mile coast from Maine to Georgia. This population was a varied aggregation of local and regional groupings, north to south and east to west, that had very little to do with, and scarcely knew, each other. The colonies themselves were long-established, economically viable, and politically stable entities that at least until the French and Indian War, had benefited from the benign neglect of the mother country. However, the population had been growing rapidly since the beginning of the eighteenth century, doubling every twenty years (thus compounding at 3.5 percent for nearly seventy years, a high rate of growth often associated today with less-developed countries).

The essential economic plan for the colonies was to clear and settle more land in order to create agricultural surpluses for export to England. This work was difficult and often hazardous, usually undertaken in remote locations with only primitive accommodations. It involved enormous front-end investment by those developing the land, and returns took years to show up in the statistics of growth rates and productivity improvements. Towns were small, markets were local at best, and most manufactured goods were imported. Though demand for skilled and unskilled labor to fulfill the theoretically unlimited economic potential of the New World was insatiable, the bulk of the population growth in colonial times came from natural increase. Immigration to the colonies was relatively modest until after the Revolution, and among the immigrants were a million or more slaves, indentured servants, transported convicts, British soldiers, officials, and agents of London merchants. Not many entrepreneurs and opportunists filled the westbound vessels looking for a chance to set up in business, but there were a few.

The inhabitants were widely dispersed across the colonies, most of them tending small farms. In 1760, nearly half of the population lived in the southern colonies, and the remainder was divided about equally between New England and the Middle Atlantic colonies. An estimated

4 percent of the population lived in one of the five largest towns in North America, most of which had already been settled for a hundred years or so. Philadelphia, then with 40,000 inhabitants, was the largest town. New York, with 25,000, was next; then came Boston with 16,000, Charleston with 12,000, and Newport, Rhode Island, with 11,000.[1] By contrast, London at the time had nearly a million inhabitants, more than 12 percent of the population of England, Scotland, and Wales combined.

All of the colonies shared some economic characteristics. They were overwhelmingly agricultural, with land, especially cleared land, serving as the principal form of capital. Though land was abundant, it had been distributed unevenly during the colonial period, and wide discrepancies were seen in the size of landholdings, especially between the northern and southern colonies. Uncleared land was relatively cheap, despite rising land prices through most of the eighteenth century, but labor to work the land was in short supply and wages for freedmen were relatively high, which discouraged tenant farming and sharecropping.

For most of the colonial period, indentured servants of one kind or another provided labor. Originally, these were persons whose transport had been paid by someone else in exchange for a contract to work for the sponsor for up to seven years to repay the debt, after which the person would be free to provide for himself. Most of the labor force was comprised of "indentured servants" of this sort, but there were others, too. A market developed for the purchase of unexpired indentures, and into this market were thrown contracts to acquire the labor of transported convicts. Benjamin Franklin recalled printing advertisements in newspapers for the sale of such contracts, a practice common in the middle 1700s. Although the unrestricted, involuntary use of the person's labor was comparable to slavery, there was little objection to the practice. African slaves, first imported in the early 1600s, were acquired for heavy farm labor from British and New England dealers, who brought them to markets in all of the principal cities, North and South. At the time of the Revolution, slavery was legal and relatively common in every colony except Massachusetts, though of course the use of slaves was greatest in the plantation colonies. In 1790, there were about 750,000 Negro slaves in North America, where they comprised about 40 percent of the population of the southern colonies.

By British rule, manufacturing was kept to a minimum in the colonies, and banks were prohibited. Nor was there any common currency in circulation. Each colony issued its own paper currency, and markets became accustomed to dealing in all sorts of coinage and paper, though the process was hardly efficient. Barter was common, especially in tobacco country, where warehouse receipts could be traded as currency. Roads were rough (though in no worse condition than the roads in Britain at the time), but they were numerous in New England and the Middle Atlantic colonies. Though overland transport was slow and awkward—especially for carrying goods—there was a postal system, designed by Benjamin Franklin, who held a valuable British appointment as deputy postmaster general for the colonies.

British capital was active everywhere in the colonies, replacing to some degree the need for local banks that mercantilist policies precluded. Returns on investments to support the tobacco and other agricultural trades, shipbuilding, fisheries, and such manufacturing as was permitted, usually was well above the cost to the lenders of the funds utilized. Adam Smith pointed out in *The Wealth of Nations* that "the greater part of both the export and coastal trade of America is carried on by the capital of merchants who reside in Great Britain. Even the stores and warehouses from which goods are retailed . . . belong to merchants who reside in the mother country."

FOUR SEPARATE ECONOMIES

Unlike England at the time of Adam Smith, the American colonies comprised four different economies spread through four distinct regions. Large labor-intensive agricultural plantations dominated the economy of the southern colonies (Maryland through Georgia), with tobacco the dominant crop. In the Middle Atlantic colonies (Delaware through New York, the most urban region), the economy was based on market farming and the activities of merchants and traders. In New England, the economy was dependent on trading, shipping, fishing, and the harvesting of forest products, particularly timber and pitch for shipbuilding. The fourth region was that of the isolated western frontier, which extended through all of the colonies once one traveled more than a hundred miles from the Atlantic coast. Trading with Indians, especially for furs, and the clearing of new land for settlement were the main economic activities.[2]

- Plantations. Tobacco was the principal cash crop of the colonies, involving about a hundred million pounds shipped to Britain in 1773, most of which was trans-shipped to the continent by British merchants. To fill this market, hundreds of farmers were involved, many with quite large plantations. British ships could sail up the Chesapeake Bay into the rivers of Virginia and Maryland then proceed right up to plantation docks. There they would load the tobacco on consignment to a London merchant and a few months later, return with a cargo of English furniture, cloth, guns, wines, and assorted fineries needed to stock and glorify the plantation and its family.

  The planter had little alternative but to trust his merchant, called a "factor," who arranged for the shipping, insurance, sorting, and reselling of the consignment into the optimal markets at the time of arrival in Europe, and the purchase, shipment, and insurance of the returning cargo. Though the factor acted as broker for the tobacco in the market (the risk of price changes remained with the planter), he would advance the planter the working capital that was needed for the coming year's crop. Once involved in all these complex relations with a tobacco factor, it was difficult for the planter to disentangle, and no doubt many found themselves paying more for these various services than they would had they known more about them, had access to competition, or had been able to purchase them individually.

But for most of the colonial period, the money was easy—all the planter had to do was deliver the crop to his own dock and everything would be taken care of. Debts to the factor, however, tended to increase if the planter was expanding his fields or his stock of imported merchandise and luxuries. As Thomas Jefferson, a big importer, said, "There was never once an instance of a man's getting out of debt who was once in the hands of a tobacco merchant and bound to consign his tobacco to him.[3] Once into such debts, the planter was obliged to increase production, which required more investment in land and slaves, or to sell off land.

Not all plantation owners were good at managing the business and many were exploited, failed to cover their costs (usually they did not understand basic accounting), and many were forced to sell or liquidate. But others were excellent businessmen. Robert Carter, one of the largest planters in Virginia, maintained a "shrewd oversight of his tobacco sales, his purchase of commodities or securities, his land transactions and the multifarious details connected with great plantations."[4] As those who were successful prospered, they learned how to manage their capital and the labor force more scientifically. They lived on the produce of their estates, optimized the use of labor and fields, and reinvested their income in additional landholdings and slaves or in different businesses. Some, like George Washington, bought extensive landholdings on the frontiers as speculations.

There were great tobacco plantations under the control of single owners in Virginia, Maryland, and North Carolina. Virginia was the largest and wealthiest colony, and it had many prominent landed families such as the Byrds, Carters, Fairfaxs, Lees, and Washingtons, with roots going back several generations. Much of Maryland, a "proprietorship" (not a colony) formed around a royal land grant to the Catholic Calvert family in 1632 by Charles I, was still controlled by members of that family. There were large plantations in the middle states, too. The Penn family still controlled much of Pennsylvania, also a proprietorship. In 1681, William Penn was granted forty-seven-million acres of forest by Charles II, in payment of a debt Charles owed to Penn's father, a prominent admiral. This may have been the largest land grant ever made to an individual not a monarch. William Penn became a Quaker and something of a social radical, and he used his powers as proprietor (unlimited power over everyone and everything in his domain) to set up a state that incorporated his liberal social ideals. Better there than here, was the sentiment of Charles. Over the years, the Penn family sold land and lost control of much of the rest, but it was still a proprietorship in 1776.

Also, in New York (which was a colony, but had grandfathered certain rights of the early Dutch settlers), Stephen Van Rensselaer, an eighth-generation descendant, owned over a million acres at the time of the Revolution. He harvested timber, fish, and furs from the parts of his properties that were not cleared for farming. According to Robert Morris, superintendent of finance for the Continental Congress, "A large portion of America is the property of great landowners, who monopolize it without cultivation."[5]

Perhaps Morris thought the landowners should be selling the land at lower prices, but that was not the way they saw it. Land was a permanent repository of value in the minds of most colonists (and Europeans). Vast accumulations should be preserved carefully, and those with funds to invest should buy land or real estate, as even careful, frugal John Adams did with his money. After

all, land prices had risen steadily over several generations, and investors had nowhere else to put their money
as neither a securities market nor bank deposits were
available to them. Land was the principal vehicle for
speculation, especially in the fertile Ohio River valley
area, disputed by the French, Indians, and two groups of
British colonists, Pennsylvanians and Virginians.

Mercantile credit and brokerage were also available to
the smaller, less conveniently located planters. This
business was sufficiently lucrative to attract a variety of
smaller brokers, who moved upriver to track down the
smaller plantation owners. On the whole, British capital
financed the tobacco trade, including the traffic in
slaves, for more than a hundred years. During the Revolution, the trade dropped off sharply, planters defaulted
on their debts, and smokers in Europe found other
sources of tobacco. After the war, cotton replaced
tobacco, and merchants from New York replaced the
British. Those of the planters who had not taught themselves business skills were still at the mercy of interme-
diaries, and found harder times ahead.

Stuart Bruchey, a historian from Michigan State and
later Columbia, studied the colonial economic system
extensively. He notes that a number of historians have
suggested that many Virginia and Maryland planters
became so dependent on outsiders that they failed to
develop the skills necessary to survive. They lived in iso-

lated, underpopulated areas well away from cities of any size. They were minimally educated, as jealous of their class, rank, and local office holdings as any English country squire, did no manual work, and subsisted on the labor of slaves. They passed on their property to eldest sons, following the English practice of primogeniture and entail, and arranged marriages so as to keep property in the family. Yet, out of this society, which apparently had far more in common with its British oppressors than with its Massachusetts co-revolutionaries, there emerged many impressive men, capable of great contributions to the new world that lay ahead of them. Among the upper-class plantation Virginians who petitioned for independence, fought in the war or held high office afterward, were Washington, Jefferson, four prominent Lees, John Marshall, several Randolphs, James Madison, James Monroe, and William Henry Harrison.

However, despite the talents of these extraordinary men (who certainly did not function only as planters), the original southern plantation owners remained backward in commercial capabilities all the way up to the Civil War and probably made a number of bad decisions about their properties. This may have been especially so concerning the acquisition and employment of slaves, never a high-return-on-investment business. Slavery involved relatively efficient markets that accurately priced the demand for labor in the emerging cotton country along the Mississippi, which drained slaves away from the much-depleted tobacco fields after the Revolution, thereby providing a decent "exit" value for eastern planters selling slaves. In any case, the simple goal of profit maximization never seemed to occur to plantation owners in the South, so in time, profits dwindled into losses, and after the Revolution, the domination of the tobacco economy of the area came to an end.

- *Farmers.* Beyond the great plantations, most colonial families in 1770, whether in the Middle-Atlantic colonies or in New England, lived at or close to subsistence level. That is, they grew their food or hunted, or made for themselves what they needed, as they carved out a living on land they owned. This land they regarded as precious, almost sacred. They or their families before them had acquired it, cleared it, put up buildings, and planted it by investing their own labor and what savings they might have had. But they were not tenants, sharecroppers, or peasants. They were landowners and as such, honorable citizens entitled to vote and hold public office. Not all of the rural population was so blessed; many had not yet earned their position as landowner, but almost all aspired to do so. They might have to labor for someone else for some years, but land was cheap enough for able-bodied, willing men and their families to acquire it in time. It was hard work, but not work for wages. Indeed, they were capitalists. They worked for themselves to create equity value in the property they owned, which could be passed on to their children. In this important sense, as farmers, they had little in common with their British and European contemporaries who did the same work, but for others.

These colonial farmers often started out with very little, barely getting by. How high above this level they might rise depended entirely on whether they could raise a surplus to exchange for manufactured goods. Most people produced some surplus, and exchanged it in local markets or with storekeepers or other merchants. Organized markets were scattered, but those living near water could reach them by boat. Some produce, like tobacco, could be used as a money crop, and bartering was common.

The principal problem for small landholders was the scarcity of markets, especially in the colonies south of the Chesapeake Bay or in the more remote locations in New England. For those in New York, New Jersey, Pennsylvania, and Delaware, the availability of markets for the exchange of produce was much more prevalent, and as a result, so too were roads, postal services and, consequently, the flow of news and information.

In a number of villages, the local inhabitants had become virtually self-sufficient as a result of internal markets wherein blacksmiths, cabinetmakers, and lawyers (such as John Adams, a self-proclaimed farmer from Braintree, Massachusetts) could exchange their services for agricultural produce or land. General storekeepers, like Connecticut's Governor Jonathan Trumbull, bartered pots and pans, gunpowder, looking glasses, furs, skins, and food. This group of colonists was less affected directly by the British economic policies than were other groups; they were unaware that their rate of economic growth might have been greater than it was except for these policies. Most were not much concerned with such policies until the imposition of taxes and the quartering of troops became issues. Then they became the new country's first bastions of defense by providing the bulk of soldiers for General Washington's army and in provisioning the troops in the field.

• *Frontiersmen.* Some small farmers lived on the frontiers. These remote areas were not the borders of their colonies (most of the land grants had no western border other than the Pacific Ocean) but the boundaries of civilized life, where you could expect to encounter Indians more easily than neighbors, and when you did, you were on your own. Some of these people were woodsmen who enjoyed the life of hunting and trapping, but many were new arrivals out to secure inexpensive land for themselves. They were devoted to one of life's most unending but ultimately rewarding endeavors: clearing forested land. They had little to do with the cash economies of the cities, only occasionally selling produce or bartering it for tools and other items they needed. Statistically, their work and important contribution to economic growth was not counted. If it had been, the colonial economic growth rate might have had to be revised upward considerably as the frontier had been an active place for significant numbers of colonists, beginning with the earliest days in Virginia and Massachusetts.

For the frontier people, improving land was their opportunity in life, the best way they knew to better themselves and make some money. Many of the small farmers outside of the market towns in 1776 were yesterday's frontiersmen. Indeed, the allure of the frontier, as rough and dangerous as it was, was a continuous problem for colonial governments. These feared that settlers would antagonize the Indian populations or clash with the French, thus requiring the colonies to defend the frontiers at considerable expense against attack or invasion.

Adam Smith made the point that the value of a man's labor could be measured either by what he might be paid for it in money or what it was able to create in the way of commodity values that might be sold in the market. This suggested that commodities might have more stable, lasting value than circulating money, but also, he added, man's (minimum) "natural wage" for his labor ought to be valued at least at what it took to sustain him and his family. Smith had the opportunity to apply his analogies to the wildernesses of colonial America. The English farmer, a tenant for some large landowner, worked for money wages. Depending on the value of the wages and the commodities he would trade for them, he might or might not earn his natural wage. If a man could not earn his natural wage at his trade, he ought to take up another, Adam Smith reasoned. Under English laws and practices, however, this was not always possible. But assuming he did so, the man would be demonstrating another of Smith's key principles—i.e., individuals are capable of determining their own economic self-interest and will act accordingly.

In the frontiersman's case, he did agricultural work, but not for wages. Instead, he took the chance that he could earn his natural wage by becoming an entrepreneur. He would invest his labor to gain the value of his improved property. For years, however, it would be hard, dangerous work; he would produce little to sell and have to subsist on what he could obtain from the land. But the value of his labor was being invested in improving his land. For this, his reward was to be a capital gain. In time, the land would be cultivated for markets and he would receive in addition an income from which he could indulge in some luxuries or otherwise invest in more land, equipment, or slaves. The wilderness farmer, in other words, was not a worker of the sort that Adam Smith studied in England. But, as Smith predicted, some people would figure out that their best interests would be met by taking their chances on the frontier; they were willing to exchange the upside value for the risks and hardships, a fairly sophisticated calculation of self-interest. That the American frontiers were filled with risk-takers for almost two hundred years gives evidence that even unschooled people can spot opportunities when they see them, and act on them when they do.

Some of the frontier families lived well inland, but not remote from towns of one sort or another; others had moved across the Alleghenies into the Ohio River valley, which was thought to contain potentially valuable farmland. Many of the large landowners in the colonies vied with each other and with the colonial governments and the government in London, over these frontier lands. Lord Fairfax, together with the royal governor of Virginia and a number of wealthy landowners, presented a petition to London asking to be assigned land in the Ohio valley. They sold shares in the newly organized Ohio Company to develop this land, and George Washington, a shrewd land speculator who knew the area well, was an investor.

It was not to be, however. After the French and Indian War, the situation on the frontier had changed. Now that the Indians were less of a threat without the French to goad them—so the colonists thought—the dreaded British army could go home. The royal government, however, did not see it that way. There were former French forts in the Ohio region that had to be manned. Then there was an Indian revolt (Pontiac's rebellion,

1763–65) that had to be put down. The British were afraid of being caught in a sinkhole, costing huge amounts of money and manpower to maintain peace on the frontier, and they decided to close it. In 1763, they declared that the eastern half of the Mississippi basin, from the river to the Appalachians (including much of the most desirable land), was reserved for Indians and therefore closed to settlement. This came just at the time when settlement fever was at its peak—trailblazing pioneers like Daniel Boone had cut their way through mountain gaps and begun to lay long-distance roadways through the West. Taxes might bother frontiersmen some, if any of them had any money or actually bothered to pay taxes, but shutting off the western opportunities to them was a serious offense indeed.

- *Traders.* In the major ports, British merchants handled trade with England, and colonial merchants handled local and coastal trade as well as some business in the West Indies, where there were many towns and harbors in which shallow-drafted vessels were preferred. Colonial merchants did a little bit of everything; they were exporters, importers, shippers, wholesalers, retailers, traders, agents, lenders, and insurers. They used their own capital to acquire goods and handled other goods on consignment or as broker. Some invested in land and other businesses, or in British securities. Some, especially once the special duties were imposed by Parliament, were also smugglers; some were slave dealers, and some traded with Indians for whiskey and firearms.

Many merchants began as sailors, visiting ports in the Caribbean, the Gulf of Mexico, and along the St. Lawrence, learning what was where. As captains, they learned to be merchants, buying and selling entire cargoes, and knowing when to sail away to another port to find a better offer. They had to know their counterparts in different ports, had to be able to handle the mathematics of trade and foreign exchange, had to understand insurance and to act in all ways as if the goods being dealt with were their own. Indeed, such captains were permitted to acquire and trade some cargo for themselves, from which they might build a stake for a business of their own, usually by buying a ship, possibly with an investment from the merchant for whom they had worked before. The British, by contrast, shipped goods across the ocean in large vessels that were met by their companies' agents on arrival, in which case, the captains usually were not given much leeway to decide commercial matters.

A successful captain might buy another ship, or several ships, and begin to operate a fleet, which often meant doing so from a headquarters in one of the port cities, where he could arrange for others to become captains. As the need for trustworthy captains could not have been greater, it was essential to engage only persons one knew well, such as relatives.

Merchants were affected by many British regulations in the colonial period, mainly those that sharply limited the availability of circulating currency, but most were able to live with or get around them. Inventories turned over slowly. Margins, many claimed, were not high, and great ingenuity and resourcefulness were necessary to provide the occasional windfall that would provide success, and to diversify against unexpected losses. Information about prices and market opportunities was crucial; some of this came from correspondents, some as a result of tips or privileges provided by colonial officials.[6] Among the most prominent and wealthy merchants at the time of the Revolution were John Hancock of Boston, who inherited an important trading firm worth £100,000 (about $12 million today) from his uncle, Thomas Hancock, in 1764; and Robert Livingston of New York; and Robert Morris of Philadelphia. Morris became the chief financial officer of the Continental Congress.

ECONOMIC GROWTH IN THE COLONIES

Adam Smith, who judged economic growth in the colonies largely by the increase in population, assumed that the colonies were growing much faster in 1776 than was Great Britain. Abundant raw materials and a labor supply increasing by immigration would in time, he reasoned, inevitably result in the colonies catching up with, and ultimately overtaking, Britain as a world economic power. (He estimated that this would take about a hundred years, and he was just about right.) Smith's judgment as to relative growth rates, however, was not based on per-capita data, which is necessary to assess relative levels of productivity and its resulting "opulence."

Although statistical data from the period hardly exists and it is difficult to prove one's point of view, many scholars have concluded (after a number of trade-offs) that the colonial rate of growth in GDP per capita before 1790 was probably less than 1 percent per year; some modern historians argue that it was around only 0.5 percent. This suggests that colonial economic growth was between one-third and two-thirds that of the independent United States in the first half of the nineteenth century. Further, colonial economic growth was probably less than, or no more than, the growth rate in Britain at the time. Smith may have had no evidence to support his idea that the colonies enjoyed a greater growth rate than England, but he might have been tempted to suggest the hypothesis to support his effort to rescind the mercantilist policies of the British government on the grounds that they were suppressing their own opportunities for wealth creation.

Certainly the mercantile system in place for generations had its intended effect to transfer much of the national wealth in America to Britain through terms of trade and payment for services. Net of returning imports of manufactured and luxury goods, colonial exports to Britain provided a trade balance from 1700–1773 of £11 million, a huge sum for the time ($1.3 billion today), according to a study by Lawrence Harper. Harper estimated that English mercantilism exploited Americans to the extent of somewhere between $2.5 million to $7 million per year at the time of the Revolution. Surely, had the colonies had the benefit of that amount of money circulating within their own economies, their growth rates might have been higher, and (a point Adam Smith made) their British owners would have been better off. A free market will allocate resources optimally for economic results.

On the other hand, the estimated per-capita cost of mercantilism ($1 to $3 per person) was not very significant and there were some benefits of British protectionism. The colonists would not be where they were except for the British, who had created, nurtured, and defended the colonies, and still did. The British were certainly entitled, so they thought, to more than a little gratitude in America for all this. But they also thought (at least King George and his ministers did) that they were entitled to the respect and obedience that the colonials owed to their landlords and their betters back in England. Besides, even if this were not so, colonists lacked the labor force and the knowledge of technology to handle large-scale manufacturing, transoceanic shipping, and the related financial services that were performed by skilled British agents. So the colonists were better off sticking to their specialties—internal trade and agriculture—which were quite adequately profitable for a great number of lower- and middle-class colonials (far greater indeed than they could expect in Britain). The colonials lacked the capital, the contacts, and the market know-how needed to succeed in international trade, so why not just leave it to the British, who were, by years of practice, better at it anyway?[7]

Despite the cost to the colonies (and, according to Adam Smith, to their British investors) of the mercantile system, there were few complaints. In 1765, James Otis published an article in the *Boston Gazette* claiming that the various restrictions on American trade were the equivalent of a "special tax on Americans" that added as much as 50 percent to the cost of British-manufactured goods bought in the colonies.[8] A decade later, when the British asked what would be necessary to reduce the tensions in the colonies, Franklin replied that for one thing, prohibitions on manufacturing would have to be removed if the colonies and the mother country were to get along better. Otherwise, the literature of the American Revolution is silent on criticisms of the underlying system of economic administration to which colonists had long been subjected. Instead, most complaints were about small taxes and their enforcement, regarded as abuses of government and the rights of Englishmen.

It is also arguable, however, that by the latter years of the eighteenth century, the accumulated economic infrastructure and growth in available skills and appetites in the colonies had almost rendered the mercantile system obsolete in America. This argument suggests that had the Revolution not occurred when it did, the system would have collapsed of its own weight. Maybe, but Adam Smith discovered how strong resistance in Parliament could be to changes or reforms that threatened the vested interests of powerful landowners and their political allies that had been in place in Britain for a century. There, it took more than fifty years for some of Smith's simplest ideas on trade and the role of government to find their way into public policy, despite wide support for them. It is likely that had the British avoided the mistakes they made in the 1760s and 1770s, the Revolution would not have occurred then. But it is also likely that it would have come later, even if the same mistakes were not made, when the cumulative weight of the mercantilists had finally become too heavy for the colonists to bear without a fight.

Besides enforcing the policies of mercantilism, the British government had other controversial roles that were important to the colonies. It promoted slavery in the southern colonies in order to increase the output of valuable agricultural commodities such as tobacco, rice, and indigo, as it had done in the Caribbean colonies. For more than a hundred years, British ships had brought slaves from Africa to America, and they continued to do so until the Revolution. Britain also exported its criminals to the colonies, where it would sell the labor of convicts to the highest bidder. It practiced

ADAM SMITH AND THE ORIGINS OF AMERICAN ENTERPRISE

the time-honored policy of recognizing the "influence" of those already occupying high "place" in British society, in the distribution of appointments or other favors of the government to friends or relatives of the well-connected, regardless of merit or ability. And in general, it looked down upon and discriminated against native-born British colonials in many ways. George Washington was much offended not to receive a commission in the royal army during the time of his service as a colonial officer in the early years of the French and Indian War. He developed a deep resentment against British arrogance and authority that certainly helped turn this comfortable Virginia planter into a rebel.

But prior to the French and Indian War, the British grip on the colonial economies had been loose, and its touch relatively light. Enforcement was not always rigorous; indeed, often it was lax. Some manufacturing was permitted, particularly that of iron smelting and casting. Mild forms of corruption allowed rules to be overlooked in exchange for bringing a government official into a deal. Some governors were in sympathy with the colonials in certain of their ventures, such as was the case with the Ohio Company. British capital could often be found if a promising project was proposed, as surely little capital was available locally. Bribes and other favors were paid on occasion for prized offices, or for business contracts with the government. The system was very laissez-faire, and the major barriers to economic growth in America were probably the many natural ones, not those of British policies. And, one might ask, what if the British were not the British, but the Dutch, Spanish, or the French, whose record of colonial administration and economic development was certainly worse than Britain's?

SOCIOLOGIES

To the British who governed the Americas, the native colonials were a separate class beneath themselves. Colonial society consisted of a large and amorphous body that began somewhere just above indentured servants and rose up the ladder to large landowners. Men of merit could succeed in this society regardless of breeding, which of course was very different from the social practices in England. A colonial might be appointed a royal governor, as Benjamin Franklin's illegitimate son William was, but that was it. There were no colonial-born members of the British peerage, no generals, no knights or privy counselors, no one to receive gratuitously great grants of land. The British simply were not interested in what happened within the colonial class, whose members were thought to be their stewards and servants. Benjamin Franklin was given an honorary doctorate by the University of Edinburgh for his scientific work, but received no acknowledgment by the king or the government, despite his great renown in Europe.

Within the large society of colonial commoners, however, there was room for upward mobility of a sort that might never have been tolerated in Britain at the time. A number of prominent Americans in the late eighteenth century had been indentured servants; one signer of the Declaration of Independence, George Taylor, came to America as an Irish transported criminal. Many stories of colonials who arrived penniless in America and ended up rich were in circulation. Benjamin Franklin's best-selling book was not *Poor Richard's Almanac,* but *The Way to Wealth,* which was a compilation of admonitions to industry, frugality, enterprise, and other virtues needed for material success.

The late-colonial period was too needy of human talent and energy to neglect any of it. People in America were acknowledged for their achievements, not for their parentage or birthplace. Though most Americans were relatively poor, they lived above the subsistence level, many owning land or property. Those willing to work were thought to be "ignorant of wants"—they could be well fed, minimally educated, and offered regular employment. This was rarely the case for the poor in England. The colonial period in the New World was a time of great opportunity for those who were poor but eager to get ahead. In time, the word got out.

Most colonials were native-born; modest levels of immigration in the eighteenth century helped population increase, but not as much as eight to ten children per family did. Though they were descended from immigrants, and immigrants themselves at heart, the large immigration booms began after the Revolution, when they brought needed skills and ambitions to the new economy. But in the period before the Revolution, the great impetus toward upward mobility, ambition, and drive for economic success was that these were not denied in America, as they were in Europe by one's church, parish or town, or by one's social betters. Every American family had an immigrant not far in its past who inspired descendants with the idea that self-improvement was available to those willing to work for it.

America was formed, many scholars have claimed, to secure religious freedom. The idea derives not only from the experience of the Pilgrims and the subsequent Puritan enclave in New England. It owes some of its credence to the early experience of the Anglicans in Virginia, the Catholics in Maryland, the Quakers in Pennsylvania, and the many sects of Protestantism that arrived afterward. These societies came to America when they were unpopular at home, and they actively promoted their religious beliefs where they settled. The different colonies had little to do with each other, and few colonists ever traveled into the realm of other religions, so coexistence was not difficult. No colony was so strong, or so motivated as to attempt to force itself upon another, even assuming that the British governors would have allowed it to do so. The colonies did depend on each other for trade, however, and the price of trade was religious and cultural tolerance. This toleration quarantined America from some economic frictions, inefficiencies, and impediments common at the time in Europe, where devout Catholics ruled one half and Protestants the other.

The Catholics were more interested in missionary work in America than in settling the place with enterprising Europeans. They had a mission to bring God's will and message to the heathens of Mexico, Peru, Cuba, and Brazil, as well as to the Indian tribes of Canada, a mission that became more difficult after the French and Indian War. The Protestant groups were mainly interested in setting up their own societies wherein they could practice the religion they believed in, and make it the law of the land where they settled. They were rarely interested in converting the savages. To Protestants, the basic idea was that the priesthood was not necessary to interpret God's teachings to man; man could do it directly. Salvation was not earned as a result of obedience to church policies and rituals; it had to be earned by one's own efforts to live a virtuous life and make the most of oneself. This one did by practicing Protestant "ethics," which consisted of (as described by Max Weber) honesty, industry, zeal, punctuality, frugality, and regularity. These virtues, first noticed by the Scotsman, John Knox, and the Swiss, John Calvin, according to Weber, advanced the interests of capitalism. They may have spread their seeds in America, too, but if so, these seeds were mixed with those from many other cultures and creeds. No religion was allowed to dominate the colonies, nor was any state religion prescribed when the Constitution was finally passed.

It is impossible therefore to give full credit to the Protestant ethic (i.e., its supposed work ethic) for setting up American capitalism. Those settlers at Jamestown did not have much of a religious agenda. Even on the *Mayflower*, the Puritans, who did have a religious agenda, were outnumbered by those who did not. Their devotion was strong enough, however, for them to attract coreligious emigrants, and they managed to enforce Puritanism for a while in the Massachusetts Bay Colony. Those who did not want to be ruled in this way migrated to Rhode Island, or New Hampshire, or to Maine, or Connecticut. But the picture of the New England "Yankee trader" derives from that of the old Puritan merchant trying to make something of himself sufficient to catch God's eye and secure a place in heaven. Later immigrants included many Englishmen, Dutch, and Germans who, though Protestants, were not Puritans.

Everyone was thrown together in the principal cities and had to find ways to get along. It worked well to create a society, which for lack of priority given to religious doctrines or social standing in a landed aristocracy, could focus its energies on surviving and improving its conditions of living. Survival and improvement were obtained only in a place like America, where hard work received its rewards—a belief that people of all religious faiths could share. We can surely value the work ethic, but there is nothing about it exclusive to the Protestants.

COLONIAL WEALTH

The chartered landlords controlling huge properties that had been granted to their predecessors were the richest people in North America before the Revolution. Many of them were British still living in England. Some, like the descendants of William Penn and the last of the Dutch patroons, Steven Van Rensselaer, were permanent residents in the colonies. Other than these, most of the large landholdings were in Virginia and other parts of the South.

George Washington was probably the wealthiest man in Virginia, having inherited substantial amounts of land and having married Martha Custis, the wealthiest woman in the colony. Washington had been a land surveyor as a youth and had a good eye for property. He was a lifetime land speculator; and at his death, he owned sizable tracts in Kentucky, Ohio, Maryland, New York, Pennsylvania, and Virginia. His estate was valued at $530,000 in 1799. All of Washington's stepchildren had died, and he left everything to Martha, including his slaves, who were to be freed at her death. Adjusted for inflation Washington's estate amounted to about $10 million, certainly not very large by today's standards of wealth. Surely he must have been worth more than that! His farm and residence at Mount Vernon alone might have been worth more—and he owned a great deal of other land much of which was known to be prime. But Washington's wealth lay not so much in current values— markets were fairly liquid for farmland, but not necessarily for undeveloped land on the frontier—but in the future values, which Washington believed in. More than most of his contemporaries, Washington put his money where his heart lay—in the risky but potentially valuable future that awaited economic development in an independent land. More than anyone in America, Washington risked his "life, fortune and sacred honor" to liberate his country from the British.

But not all landowners did so well. The Penn estate was largely disbursed by the time of the Revolution. The Quaker experiment in liberal government and gentle philosophies, having succeeded for a time, fell apart after William Penn's historical connections with the Stuarts and his poor business practices marked him for trouble when the British throne passed to William and Mary in 1688. Steven Van Rensselaer, probably the wealthiest native-born American when the Revolution began (he was then twelve), was unable to hold his feudal estate together once the principles of democracy reached his tenants. He was a true believer in the new country, a liberal in ways unheard of by his predecessors, and was lenient in collecting rents. On his death, he divided his property equally among his ten children rather than following the British practice of primogeniture, in which all goes to the eldest son to keep the family fortune together. After his death, his tenants rose up demanding that the estate's land be sold to them, which it was. By fifty years later, the entire million acres had been broken into parcels and sold.

John Hancock was another of America's richest men in the colonial period. He, too had risked everything in the Revolution. He was president of the Continental Congress when it passed the Declaration of Independence, and his signature appears in extra-large letters—so, he said, "the British could see it." He was one of the wealthiest merchants in New England, having inherited a success-ful whale-oil and shipping business from his uncle. The uncle had started out poor, struggled in the publishing busi-ness for a while, then married the daughter of a rich mer-chant (then possible only in a classless place like Boston). He became a supplier to the British governor and the gov-ernment, and is reported to have made most of his money from contracts with them as well as from speculation in British government securities. The business that John Han-cock took over, however, did not fare well because of the declining trade with Britain, the immediate effects of the Stamp Act, and subsequent restrictions on commercial activity.

Hancock turned to smuggling, and one of his ships, the *Liberty,* was seized by the British. Hancock was charged by the government and became a symbol of the British abuse of Yankee tradesmen. He was defended by Sam Adams, the future organizer of the "Sons of Liberty" (a son of *Liberty*?), and acquitted. The event turned Hancock to revolution, a cause he supported generously, though his shipping business failed in 1775. After the war, he served nine terms as governor of Massachusetts. He died in 1793, leaving an estate the estimated value of which was about $350,000. This was probably less than the value of the estate he inherited. It was not easy to manage a business during the Revolution and the depressed years that followed it. It took cunning and skill to do so, qualities not always found in those who inherit great wealth.

Despite difficulties, Hancock managed to leave a substantial estate, while his contemporary, Robert Morris, a shrewd, successful and much respected self-made merchant from Philadelphia, did not. Morris was born in England, came to Maryland at thirteen, and was orphaned at fifteen. He was made for business, though, and prospered on his own. He was a member of the Continental Congress during the Revolution and elected its superintendent of finance. He was extensively—more than anyone else—involved with financing the war effort in whatever way possible, often against desperate odds. Though Morris openly used his position to speculate for his own account during the war, he was considered honest, capable, and the leading businessman of his time. He was a founder of the Bank of North America, one of the first banking institutions formed in the new country. But he ended up in debtor's prison in Philadelphia in 1790, the result of a failed real estate scheme. Washington visited him there.

Benjamin Franklin, the most famous entrepreneur of colonial times, was also a wealthy man by colonial standards. Franklin might have been far richer had he been able to secure lasting patents on his many ingenious inventions, or to sell shares in his businesses—he founded the first insurance company in America and ran a successful publishing firm for many years. He was also the best-selling author of his time— thousands of copies of *Poor Richard's Almanac, The Way to Wealth,* and his *Autobiography* were sold. These books circulated in many languages and across many continents during his lifetime, but his entitlements were not protected by copyright. He symbolized the idea of the self-made man and the quiet, honorable dignity of trade that should be pursued with industry, thrift, and frugality. He was a world-renowned scientist, and a diplomat who participated in all of the events of the American Revolutionary period from the mid 1750s until his death in 1790, leaving an estate of $150,000.

CHAPTER 3

―――•◦•―――

WAR AND INDEPENDENCE

The thirteen years between Lexington and Concord and the ratification of the Constitution in 1788 were certainly some of the most anxious and crucial in America's history. During this time, the Revolution had to be financed, fought, and won—against very long odds—and then the country prevented from collapsing into the chaos of mob rule. The first eight years of the Revolution were spent at war with the world's most formidable military power, which the colonists had provoked into the embarrassing task of putting down a rebellion of defiant, ungrateful countrymen. The mutiny angered the king, George III, and he stubbornly insisted on its suppression. Kings, of course, are not supposed to tolerate revolts. The king's position fueled domestic politics in Britain and divided Parliament into the king's party, the Tories, and the opposition Whigs. The Tories were in power, however, and Lord North was the prime minister, responsible for putting down the rebellion. The trouble was, to do that, the British would have to destroy the valuable colonies they wished to preserve.

In the end, it was the long run of British blunders and misjudgments more than American valor that decided the issue. The British government acted oppressively, despite considerable resistance from the Whigs and few signs that the policy was working. Its persistence also caused the war to widen and involve three powerful global opponents— France, Holland, and Spain—forcing the government to disperse British forces in order to defend its valuable West Indian sugar islands and its far-flung holdings in India, Africa, and the Mediterranean. Further, the war risked reversing the favorable outcome of the French and Indian War, only just ended, in which Canada and Florida had been won. To these strategic negatives were added a series of humiliating tactical defeats at Saratoga, Trenton, York-town, and at sea at the hands of John Paul Jones. Finally, after Britain had tolerated these results and the failed policies of the king's government for many years, the Tories were forced out and a Whig government came in that negotiated terms with the Americans—but even then, arrogantly and uncooperatively. All this took years to accomplish, and the many effects felt in America of the revolutionary time ran deep.

WAR AND TRANSITION

To begin with, the war—as all wars are—was very expensive for both sides. The British spent over £100 million (approximately $12 billion today), possibly fifty to a hundred times the amount they might have gathered from the taxes they were so determined to collect. But the British had the money, or could get it. The Americans, however, had no money to spend, but they still had to endure the crushing cost of furnishing arms, munitions, food, clothing, and the other endless requirements of wartime. They had to do this or there could be no resistance, no revolution.

The Americans began the effort with no weapons except their hunting rifles, and no magazines or powder works. They had no artillery, no ships, no factories or arsenals, or any of the means of waging war that were needed immediately. What they needed they would have to capture, purchase, or smuggle in undetected by the British fleet. From the beginning, the Americans' economic base was small, and now it was getting smaller. Ports were blockaded and trade of all kinds was sharply curtailed. The British destroyed or seized a lot of American property, much of it in cities, but more devastatingly in the countryside—where they burned farms, destroyed animals, and ran off slaves, indentured servants, and anyone else working there. Farmers were deprived of food and shelter for themselves, their families and neighbors, and for soldiers from both sides, who demanded it. Every story of home life during these times is filled with reports of desperate shortages, hunger, disease, and the death of American civilians. The common experience of such suffering hardened the determination of the American patriots.

But not all Americans were patriots. Some were loyalists. Historians have estimated that at the beginning of the Revolution, a third of the population were ardent supporters, a third opponents, and a third undecided. The early years forced them to make up their minds, and many decided to leave. About a hundred thousand American loyalists (5 percent of the white population) left the country, taking their money, their goods, and their precious skills with them to Canada or back to England. As a percentage of the total population, this was a much larger emigration than occurred during the French Revolution.[1] However, there were many loyalists who remained to assist the British or to profit from their presence. Some in New York helped supply General Clinton and his forces there. Others joined in the fighting, assisting General Cornwallis in the Carolinas in his search-and-destroy missions. The British tactics in the field, however, were so harsh and brutal that they won over to the American cause many who had begun the war with faint hearts or undecided minds.

The rebellion effectively ended American trade with Europe in tobacco and other commodities, and of manufactured goods of all kinds. Without trade, the real economy collapsed, though a "gray" market, sustained by smuggling and homemade manufactures, survived. Barter returned, but so too did the people's willingness to live at standards not much above subsistence. Though the Americans sought foreign loans, they were nearly impossible to obtain until France and Holland, whose indirect support for the Americans had provoked the British into war with them, joined the conflict after the first significant American victory, at Saratoga in 1777.

These severe disadvantages, however, were to some extent offset by some gains directly attributable to the wartime circumstances. The property of the emigrants was confiscated, and debts to English merchants and bankers were ignored. Americans, resentful of the conduct of the British that reached ever deeper into their daily lives, became more energetic and resourceful. American merchants were able to use their connections in the Caribbean to trade tobacco, lumber, rice, and indigo for large quantities of weapons and gunpowder, which were then smuggled into the country through countless bays and inlets.

The first nation to recognize the new republic was Holland, which did so in the autumn of 1776 at St. Eustatius, the principal Dutch trading port in the Caribbean. Trading with both sides in a war of this sort was lucrative business, and not only Dutch and French, but also English firms participated in it.[2] The Dutch were particularly eager to have the American business and persisted in the trade despite increasing British pressure. Ultimately, the British declared war on the Dutch, after which St. Eustatius was leveled by the British fleet. In the early days of the war, however, before the French and Dutch became involved directly, the vigorous efforts of the Caribbean traders to meet the Americans' needs kept the rebellion alive.

Ingenuity was mothered by necessity many times during the war. In January 1776, Henry Knox, a colonel in Washington's army (and a former Boston bookseller), was sent to Lake Champlain in the middle of winter to haul back, over the snow-covered Berkshire Mountains, more than fifty great artillery pieces that had been captured by Ethan Allen at Fort Ticonderoga. The guns were needed urgently for the siege of Boston, and having been put on special sleds, they arrived on time. Across the country, local workshops were turning into manufacturing centers engaged in smelting, forging, and casting iron into weapons, and making gunpowder. Sturdy oceangoing frigates were constructed for the first time for the new American navy.

Washington and his army were resourceful, too. Crossing the Delaware on Christmas night in 1776 to surprise the enemy at Trenton and win the first skirmish of the war was necessary for the nation's morale. The war, however, had just begun and there was a long way to go. Washington, aided chiefly by Robert Morris, the Philadelphia merchant, had to keep the army intact long enough to win. This was a difficult challenge; Morris used all his entrepreneurial skills to secure provisions and equipment, wheeling and dealing in whatever ways were possible. Innovative guerrilla tactics at sea with privateers, and on land with mounted raiders, captured a lot of the enemy's supplies. The term "Yankee ingenuity" owes much to this period of American history.

Enlistments were hard to come by after the first year, and desertions and mutinies became exasperatingly common. But much of Washington's small army (never more than twenty-five-thousand at one time) was hard core. Many soldiers had enlisted for the duration of the war, and before it was over, they would have participated in fifteen or more battles. Some, of course, were killed or wounded (the casualty rate was about 5 percent of those who served), or stricken by disease, and many had to tend to crops at harvest time or their families would starve. But there was always an army, and it marched and moved as it was asked to, and it was the last one standing at the end. Only with the utmost in resourcefulness, through all ranks, could the army have been sustained. Pluck, grit, and endurance, yes, but this heroic time showed something else—a respect for the importance of a common goal, a shared enterprise that individuals felt they had a duty to support. This was a new way of thinking for these former colonists.

Finally, after a year's hesitation when the morale in the country was at its lowest, the French came in and the war was effectively ended in a great victory at Yorktown. But this was no simple operation either. The original plan was for the French to ally with Washington to take New York in the summer of 1781. Instead, the French Admiral de Grasse announced in mid-August that he would arrive in the Chesapeake Bay and stay there for two months, no more, before sailing back to the Caribbean, where he was needed. Washington had to move his entire army (then about five thousand exhausted men, plus artillery and horses) 450 miles in the worst of summer heat on the Chesapeake, to join up with the French forces before they sailed away unused. Money had to be raised for the effort, especially for back pay of the troops. Because there were insufficient boats on the Delaware or at the head of the Chesapeake, the troops had to walk, and they had to be provisioned along the way. Fortunately, it all came together as it needed to. The Americans made the trek in six weeks and the French arrived on schedule. This in itself was a miracle considering the vagaries of weather and the French, and the fact that a large British fleet suddenly appeared in the Chesapeake just as the French fleet was unloading its troops. By chance, this was not the formidable fleet commanded by Admiral George Rodney in the Caribbean (he was ill), but British ships of a smaller unit dispatched from New York that turned away when de Grasse responded to the challenge.

Thus Washington was able to rendezvous with the French forces, and also with the American General Nathanael Greene, whose forces had been fighting British forces under General Cornwallis in the Carolinas. Cornwallis apparently understood the situation that was developing, but he did not try to escape the trap that was forming around him. For the Americans, everything came together just when it had to, against huge odds to the contrary. When Cornwallis was at last outnumbered, outgunned, boxed in, and trapped, he surrendered in October 1781. Washington gave a lot of credit for the victory to "Providence" for having favored the American cause. Maybe it did. The long-shot victory decided the war for the Americans.

A few years earlier, when Adam Smith had been asked to give advice to the Lord North government on the American situation, he provided a long memorandum reviewing various options, already covered in *The Wealth of Nations*. One of these options concerned union with Britain, an idea that Franklin had put forward and that now, during the war, seemed out of the question. No one, Smith claimed, but "a solitary philosopher like myself could support" the idea of union, as if nothing else had happened. However, he also expressed doubt about the likelihood of an outright military victory. Normally, a professional standing army should have little trouble subduing a mere militia, but the longer the war went on, he said, this was less likely to hold true, as both the French and Indian War and the battle at Saratoga had demonstrated. Thus he was able to imagine a military situation in which a stronger Britain could not win against a determined local population that was defending its home—unless Britain expended far more in time, money, and manpower than the colonies were worth to the Crown.

However, even if the British won, Smith added, they would lose, because military victory would have to be accompanied by a harsh, expensive occupation, in which the troops would continue to confront "factious, mutinous, and discontented subjects . . . at all times disposed to rebel." The alternative favored by Smith was to end the war, part as good friends, let the Americans have their independence, and assist them in it to "secure a natural affection of the colonies to the mother country, which perhaps our late dissentions have well nigh extinguished." However, he did note that either British military defeat or voluntary withdrawal was consistent with a fine piece of Machiavellian policy: If Canada should be restored to France, and Florida to Spain, we should "render our [former] colonies the natural enemies of those two monarchies and consequently, the natural allies of Great Britain."[3]

Smith's arguments were those used by the Whigs in the finally successful effort to bring down the Tory government. After Yorktown, the fighting persisted for another two years. When it finally ended, in September 1783, the Treaty of Paris affirmed American independence and doubled the size of the new country by setting the western border at the Mississippi, much to the delight of the frontier settlers and the land speculators. But the treaty would have to be defended, even so. The British dragged their feet in evacuating their troops from some of the forts around Detroit. And they attempted to limit American trade with Britain and its colonies in the West Indies, and continued to impress American seamen. Nor were the Spanish (allies of the French) much better. They regained control of Florida after the war and still ruled New Orleans and the Mississippi, where they restricted American trade. Because few European countries thought the Americans could defend themselves effectively, they judged the new nation to be an easy target.

Adam Smith was very conscious of the importance of national defense and believed that it ranked near the top of all priorities of government. It is "the first duty of a sovereign," he said, "to defend the society from the violence and injustice of . . . other societies." He considered standing armies essential for providing this protection, though he noted in *The Wealth of Nations* that "Men of republican principles have been [suspicious] of a standing army as [being] dangerous to liberty" with good reason. However, he added, standing armies grow progressively more expensive and must be maintained in both war and peace. Some liberal economic policies, too, even important ones, would have to cede priority from time to time to the requirements of assuring the national defense. This was a harsh message to the newly independent American states, which, after eight years of war, lacked the resources, and perhaps the will, to divert further taxes and manpower to defense requirements. Yet, the external dangers to the new republic were many.

The French dissolved into a revolution of their own in 1789, partly brought on by the expense of their support for the American cause. Its continuing protection of American interests could no longer be counted on. Indeed, French forces began to menace American trade and ships, and in 1798, a three-year "undeclared" naval war with Napoleon's post-revolutionary government broke out.

After the American Revolution, Britain continued to treat its former colonies with contempt and aggression. Its ongoing interference with trade, impressment of American sailors, and harassment of American naval ships resulted in a declared war in 1812. But the United States was prepared neither militarily nor financially to go to war with either France or Britain. It finessed the French by acquiring the Louisiana Territory, but it had to fight the British—successfully at sea, but less successfully on land. The British occupied the new city of Washington, D.C., and burned it to the ground, but the Battle of New Orleans, won by Andrew Jackson in 1815, turned the tables and convinced the British that their hopes to regain control of the Mississippi (and thus of America) were gone forever.

The revolutionary war was a great experience for most Americans. Their new country had achieved victory over a powerful opponent, at the cost of great hardship, effort, and financial loss, and all Americans were now free of whatever oppression they had felt themselves to be under. Veterans of the fighting carried their self-confidence, their experience of ingenuity and adaptability, home with them after the war, never to view their country again as they had before the war. Many of them also carried script for back pay and promises of land grants with them. For those who needed the money urgently, the script proved to be nearly worthless. For those who held on to it, trusting the government to redeem its promises, the interminable delay in doing so was disappointing. Some were forced to sell (or were tricked into selling) their claims for much less that they would one day be worth.

Still, the 200,000 or so men who fought and won the Revolution never forgot what they had done. It changed their lives like almost no other experience could. They had had their strength and courage tested, had become accustomed to some discipline, and had learned that the common good was a worthy goal to fight for. They were the first generation of free Americans, unlike any others who had come before them. They went back to their farms and businesses and rebuilt them. But it took a long time for the income of the average American to return to what it had been in 1775, though the economy varied in different regions of the new country, the South suffering in proportion somewhat more than others.

With victory came a recession and a flood of other problems. Tobacco as an export crop was almost finished. The years of warfare had ruined most of it in Virginia and North Carolina, and European buyers felt encouraged to find crops elsewhere. The agriculture-dependent American economy was in shambles and desperate for trade. The British were smugly unhelpful, denying American ships entry to Britain, Canada, and British possessions in the West Indies. French and Dutch trade did not immediately fill in for the missing British markets. Efforts to open new markets in the Mediterranean ran afoul of the notorious Barbary pirates, who demanded huge "tribute" (payoffs) to allow free passage of American ships. Before the Revolution, Britain's annual tribute payments of $280,000 covered its colonies, but not afterward.[4] American representatives abroad, such as John Adams, then in Britain striving to open the ports, were unable to negotiate on behalf of the country because the Articles of Confederation (passed in 1781) did not empower Congress to regulate commerce. The interval between the end of the war and the establishment of the new federal government in 1789 was an uncertain and difficult period.

Even so, victory over the British forced some far-reaching social and economic changes. The royal land grants in Pennsylvania, Maryland, and Virginia were canceled. Land west of the Alleghenies was now open for settlement. The mercantile restrictions on trade, finance, manufactures, and public works of all types, which had helped to keep the colonies dependent on Britain, were abolished. A merchant marine could develop, as could banks and other financial institutions. Canals and roadways to improve inland transportation could now be established. British tax collectors and their troops had gone. Each state was in the process of adopting a constitution of its own for democratic self-government that ensured a host of individual rights. A great deal had certainly changed in America when the British signed the Treaty of Paris.

Immigration during the war had dropped and was no longer available to replace the British officials and loyalists who departed, and so the population contracted for a while. However, during the first twenty years after the Revolution, the population continued to expand rapidly, mainly by natural increase, and with the arrival of about 250,000 individuals who could not resist the opportunity to try their luck early in the new country. The French Revolution and the continental wars with Napoleon that began in 1793 probably attracted some European emigrants and kept others out until 1815. A number of skilled British merchants and bankers appeared in the United States to set up business operations, including David Parish of Baring Brothers, who settled in Philadelphia in 1805,[5] and Alexander Brown & Sons, and Oliver & Thompson, who were in Baltimore.[6] By 1800, the total population of the United States was 5.3 million (including one million Negro slaves), a 36-percent increase from 1790.

Immediately after the war, American government finances were a mess. The various paper currencies in circulation were virtually worthless. Revenues from trade were sparse, and manufacturing efforts had to be shifted from war materials to other goods. Both British and American claims for unpaid debts and confiscated property were dismissed, but not until the Treaty of Paris. Victories at Saratoga and Yorktown had made it possible to secure some foreign loans, but the immediate prospects for repaying them were dim. The Continental Congress continued as the only organ of government other than the individual states, which were reluctant to cede it any powers. Discontent was rising, and dissatisfaction with the continental government led to protests in various cities. A revolt over taxes and the unfair treatment of veterans led to Shay's Rebellion in Massachusetts in 1786. Most of the founding fathers of 1776 wrote of the disappointment and discouragement they felt when they saw the unrest in the country they had risked so much to create.

CREATING A NEW GOVERNMENT

A new functioning republic had to be launched, one that could aspire to the goals of the Revolution only by surviving and prospering, unlike all those other republics who had declared independence and had never been heard of again. It was obvious that the weak, patchwork system of government put together during the war under the Articles of Confederation would not suffice for the larger, more vulnerable country that emerged after the Treaty of Paris. However, by the time the Constitutional Convention was first called (1787), there had been time to consider the underlying legal structure needed to support the political and economic goals of the Revolution. And during the interregnum between the end of the war and the signing of the Constitution, there had been time to gain a clear picture of what the cost of failing to agree on a new system would be—the revolutionary effort would surely fail.

There had also been time for a new generation of leaders, intellectuals, and men of affairs, rather than political revolutionaries and warriors, to emerge, eager to shape and mold the new structure. Only a few of the representatives to the Constitutional Convention, including Benjamin Franklin and Robert Morris, were signers of the Declaration of Independence; only a few, including George Washington, were former army generals. Jefferson and Adams were abroad, though colleagues kept them both well informed.

The fifty-five representatives to the Convention were appointed by the state legislatures and were expected to meet stringent property-holding tests that each state, to different degrees, had established for high political office. Almost all were men of education and prominence, many also of considerable wealth. None were interested in any form of popular democracy, which they would have considered mob rule. Also, almost all of them had significant economic interests in the outcome of their work. One reason they were successful, perhaps, is that those who attended the Constitutional Convention and participated in their endless discussions were themselves users of government, not providers of it. They searched for ideas and studied the best of them.

There were basically four economic spheres of interest associated with the framing of the Constitution. First there were the common folk—the farmers, laborers, and craftsmen, comprising the majority of the population. Many of them held Confederation paper for services during the war. They did not like paying taxes, but in fact, they paid few of them at the time. Their main interests lay in the formation of a system that would permit real economic growth. No one among the representatives at the Convention could be said to be from this section of the population.

In fact, all of the delegates had reason to be distrustful and suspicious of mob behavior, having seen much of it during the Revolution. They probably would have agreed on one thing—the best way to lose the new republic would be to introduce common democracy, in which mobs could gain control of political offices and the powers contained in them. If that should happen, the government would effectively destroy itself, or cause a tyrant to appear. This they believed to be the history of all previous republics. (This was not quite right—Holland and Switzerland were more or less republics at the time—but it was what most believed anyway.) The delegates, all sober men of substance, had not fought against a British tyrant to replace him with one of their own. The example of the French Revolution was just around the corner, but like Adam Smith, even then they could remember Julius Caesar and Oliver Cromwell.

After the common folk were the merchants, manufacturers, and shippers, all of whom believed it was essential that trade and reasonable economic order be resumed as quickly as possible. They also wanted a navy to protect their ships, industrialization promoted, and protective tariffs adopted to keep out lower-priced, foreign-manufactured goods. Eleven delegates were from this sector. The existing Continental

Congress of course had no powers to do anything about trade, finance, a navy, or industrialization.

Next there were the large landowners and large and small speculators, who had much interest in the future of the new land from the Alleghenies to the Mississippi, which was now held (and disputed) by the states. The Articles of Confederation gave no power to Congress to resolve border disputes between states, which had become numerous as states absorbed land granted to absent Britons. Conflicting claims to western boundaries and land purchased from the Indians grew. Those with great plantations, the tobacco growers in the South and the New York patroons, worried about the effect of the Revolution, and its spirit of equality and liberation, on their slaves and tenant farmers. There were at least fourteen representatives with significant land interests at stake, and fifteen representatives were significant slave owners.

Finally, there were the financial people, those who owned or dealt in securities, loans, and other forms of monetary traffic. Twenty-four representatives were bankers, money dealers, or investors in interest-bearing paper. Forty were persons whose names later appeared in the records of the Treasury Department as owning or transacting in "government securities."[7] This was the paper issued during and since the Revolution by the states, and the Continental paper issued to pay for war supplies and to cover soldiers' wages. The market value of this paper, however, was low, sometimes only five cents on the dollar. There was no power in Congress under the Articles of Confederation to raise taxes or to manage national financial obligations, and the states were unwilling to act. There was no such thing as a central fiscal or monetary policy. The country operated as if it were in a self-imposed state of bankruptcy, but one without a court system to help resolve it. Under the Articles of Confederation, few payments were made on the debt, and there was little hope for any. Things just bumped along as best they could, but there was virtually no credit, and financial assets were depreciated as no one could afford to place confidence in them.

So a lot had to be done by the delegates to produce a system that would guarantee the goals of the Revolution, be accepted as fair to all classes and interest groups, and be efficient in execution so that the country would be able to govern itself. All this required an enormous amount of work, argumentation, and persuasion. Emphasis had to be placed on practical measures that everyone could understand and agree on, not on abstract theories, no matter how brilliant the theorists.

The brightest stars of this period were Alexander Hamilton, John Jay, and James Madison, who contributed enormously to the debates related to the principal constitutional issues and published many of their arguments in *The Federalist Papers.* At forty-two, Jay was the oldest when the debates began in 1787. The three men read everything they could about modern (and ancient) governments. They fed at the tables of the Enlightenment until they were gorged. They read Voltaire, David Hume, and the speeches of Edmund Burke, Charles James Fox, and the elder William Pitt, the great English statesman who vigorously opposed the king and his government's American policies. They also read Adam Smith's *The Wealth of Nations*. They were looking for good ideas they could put to work in America. They were not looking for ways to refine the British or the French models of government in which political and economic power went only to a select few. Though they agreed that the British system of a parliamentary monarchy (as opposed to an absolute monarchy) had produced the most successful political-economic system in the world for generating national wealth and power, they confidently thought they could do better. While they were conscious of designing a system for balancing political power in an overlapping federal-state apparatus, they may not have been conscious of designing with it an effective economic system.

But their awareness may have been increased after consulting the works of Adam Smith closely. Opulence, he said, is greatest when the underlying economic system that supports it is efficient. But no economic system can work efficiently that is not essentially just, he added. It is obviously inefficient to have an unjust system that must be enforced at great cost. That means that any laws that allocate powers, subsidies, monopolies, kickbacks, and other benefits to just a chosen few, or otherwise abuse and suppress the laboring classes, should be discarded, as they could be neither just nor efficient. And if opulence is to be maximized for the greater benefit of *everyone* in the system, the government's role in allocating economic resources must be minimal but potent. Governments should encourage the growth of free markets, in which prices are set by the interaction of supply and demand, and to aid the private sector in matters it cannot easily do for itself, such as provide for public services (like road building) and for the national defense. If the government voluntarily gives up the old monarchial powers and entitlements that meddle with the national wealth, trusting instead in the invisible hand, it will be led to a state of optimal resource allocation. Of course, in the event of overriding concerns, such as a call to defense, deviations from the model may be appropriate, but only as long as there is a threat to the country.

Thus the essential teachings of Adam Smith were that the lightest hand of government would create the greatest amount of opulence. Such a laissez-faire approach was in direct contrast to everyone's former experience of government. For people of the eighteenth century, this line of thinking was new, radical, and most likely regarded as uncertain and dangerous. It took courage to even consider such a system.

In any event, a determined self-confidence, led a small group of men in their thirties and forties to think they could design a new constitutional system of republican government that would perform better than the monarchial system that had produced the world's strongest and richest powers. Possibly some bolstering of that confidence came from the quiet teachings of the dry, distant Scottish academic who encouraged a different way of thinking about government. It had, Adam Smith said, an economic purpose as well as a political one—and in the long run, the economic results, more profoundly than the political, would determine the system's success. Smith was very persuasive, but then, what he was saying to them was exactly what they wanted to hear.

The three authors of *The Federalist Papers* thus bought into Adam Smith's reasoning, but they knew that *The Wealth of Nations* was aimed at reforming the highly successful British economic system, not at creating a new economic republic. Their struggle was to balance the political and economic powers of a new central government with the distributed local powers of the constituent states that made up the republic. They wanted the federal government to have sufficient powers to be effective and the states to retain sufficient powers to feel safe from encroachment by other states. The issue rested on the degree of power allotted to the central part, especially insofar as powerful economic forces were concerned.

The common people under the new American Constitution, the Federalists claimed, need not fear a heavy-handed central government that controlled (and exploited) all economic activity, nor one that allocated precious resources to the pockets of a few favorites. All economic power in the end rested in the Congress, the members of one house of which were elected by the public. But, that being true, could property owners, businessmen, and financiers still be at peace with the new system? "Yes," said Hamilton and the others in *The Federalist Papers*.[8] The inviolability of private property was essential to any economic system, especially in a market economy. Under the Constitution, private property would be protected by law from the natural instincts of a large, democratically enfranchised population to expropriate it. But equally, anyone's property would be so protected, even a foreigner's. Anyone could come into the country and enter into any profession, trade, or occupation and succeed or not, based entirely on one's own merits and luck, and expect to retain the money he had made. Everyone would have the same chance, or, in other words, the chances for success could be no worse than random. For many in Europe, this seemed to be a big improvement in the odds.

The American Constitution defers to market forces to an extraordinary degree, without overtly attempting to do so. The government cannot spend money (or tax to get it) without the consent of the elected members of Congress—

i.e., both the House (common men) and the Senate (powerful oligarchs from the states)—and the approval of the executive. The process involved in achieving any legislation (in which it is easier to deny a law than to create one) makes it difficult to favor any one interest group all the time. Creating a new federal law is something of a free-market process in itself, in which the demand for supporting votes has to be met by the supply. Certainly the congressional representatives will trade off with each other and maneuver to support or kill off a proposed bill, but that is part of a market process, too, insofar as their votes are reflective of the people who elected them. In any case, when the legislature overdoes it, the judiciary has power to revoke laws that are not consistent with the intent of the Constitution, thus providing a level playing field for everyone.

In economic terms, this meant that the laws controlling commercial competition in America must survive such a constitutional process, which would insulate them from patronage or favor or influence from government officials or powerful citizens outside the government. When commerce is forced to work in this way, competition will function on the basis of economic merit and delivery of customer value. Investments allocated to the most competitive parts of the system should receive the highest returns, the objective of all investors. Thus, under the constitutional system, the allocation of national resources, capital, and labor is mainly the result of market forces, all to the public good and the greater creation of opulence. Adam Smith never wrote about his opinions of the U.S. Constitution (he died in 1790, at age sixty-seven, only two years after it was ratified), but from reading what he did write, we have much reason to believe he would have approved.

Of the three American constitutional stars, according to historian Charles Beard, "*The* colossal genius of the new system" was Alexander Hamilton, thirty-two years old when the Convention began. "Though he had little part in the formation of the Constitution, his organizing ability made it a real instrument bottomed on the substantial interests of the time. . . . He perceived that governments were not made out of thin air and abstract principles. He knew that the Constitution was designed to accomplish certain definite objects, affecting in its operation certain definite groups of property rights in society. He saw that these interests were at first inchoate, in process of organization, and he achieved the task of completing their consolidation and attaching them to the federal government."[9]

Not only that, but as the country's first secretary of the treasury, Hamilton was there to execute the policies and set the precedents that would link the support of basic economic integrity to the new federal system of government in the United States. Without Hamilton, however poorly it may have operated at times, the federal system might not have been able to survive the many tests placed upon it.

But it has survived, fundamentally unchanged since the days of the Constitutional Convention, mainly because the system worked and powerful precedents for the economic management of government were established at the beginning and held to ever since.

IMPLEMENTING A CONSTITUTION

Alexander Hamilton was an extraordinary man whose talents fit his times. He was born in the British West Indies, the illegitimate son of a failed Scottish businessman. He was orphaned at thirteen, apprenticed as a clerk to a local shipping company whose owner soon allowed him a free hand in running the operation. This man and some other local citizens financed Hamilton's trip to America in 1773 to secure an education, which he obtained at King's College (now Columbia) after rejecting Princeton because it refused to admit him as a student with advanced standing. Soon afterward, he was caught up in the revolutionary fervor, joining a New York militia company as a junior artillery officer. Like a lot of people of his time with no family background or connections, he saw advancement opportunities for himself in a war. He served in the army from its beginning, as an aide to George Washington and in the field. He was at the Battle of Long Island, at Trenton, at Valley Forge, and at Yorktown, where as a colonel, he was chosen to capture one of two important redoubts held by the British. After the war, he returned to New York, became a lawyer and helped found the Bank of New York in 1784, when he was twenty-nine. As a delegate to the Constitutional Convention and an active participant in the debates, he taught himself all he could about governments, then rejected most of it.

A highly pragmatic man, Hamilton believed that great men of action achieved the results they did because of the experience they had accumulated and their willingness to jump in and get things done. Equally, he was disinclined to accept theories and abstract ideas, however engaging, if they came from isolated academics or others remote from what he considered the real world. Having no regional association in the country, he could see it more clearly as a whole than many others. He became the predominant spokesman for strong federal government and formed around him the Federalist political party to support this belief. The opposition was the Republican party—formed and led by Thomas Jefferson and his protégé James Madison, Hamilton's former *Federalist Papers* co-author—who wanted a weaker federal government, one that would lack powers to interfere with government by the states. As treasury secretary, Hamilton introduced landmark proposals for restoring the credit, for establishing a central bank, and for encouraging manufacturing.

Hamilton was vain, ambitious, extremely touchy, and

wary of insult, and he became the subject of the first government sex-and-money scandal. He did not lie about it, however, and accordingly he was subjected to public humiliation and vilification, though cleared of any financial improprieties. He left office before Washington's term was up and returned to New York, where he became heavily involved in politics. He was appointed, on Washington's advice, as major general and second in command of the U.S. Army in 1798, when the old general was called back to defend the country against an expected invasion by the French that never materialized. Hamilton was fiercely partisan, a power broker who actively influenced the selection of both John Adams and Thomas Jefferson as Presidents. In 1804, Hamilton was killed in a duel with Jefferson's vice president, Aaron Burr (whom he had opposed), at the age of forty-nine.

Alexander Hamilton was treasury secretary from September 1789 through January 1795. While in office, he dealt with a number of important precedent-setting issues early on as an executive of the government and a defender of the Constitution. Of all of President Washington's cabinet, something of an all-star list at the time, Hamilton's actions are unique in historical importance. In addition to near bankruptcy, no currency, no sources of national revenue, no monetary or fiscal system, the government was facing the war debt, crushing amounts of it, which had left the country with no sources of credit. Despite the bravery of the Americans in the Revolution and the elegance of its Declaration of Independence and Constitution, the effort to create a new country would be in vain unless its financial condition could be quickly rectified. "Third world" countries had been invaded even before the 1780s by creditor nations seeking to collect their debts. Others had been forced to give up their sovereignty in trade for credit. Hamilton was well aware that what spoils the British could not get in one way, they might try to grab by another.

The first important issue for Hamilton as treasury secretary was to decide the fate of all the government debt, which was paper then trading at large discounts, much of which had already changed hands, forcing the original owners to realize losses. The discounts were grist for speculators before and immediately after the Constitution was ratified. They bought up the paper cheaply, expecting (or hoping) that the federal treasury would redeem it at par. Hamilton proposed a plan for the federal government to do this by assuming the debts of the Continental Congress *and* of the various states. Assumption of state debts was very contentious—the debt burden (mostly for the war) had not fallen evenly; some states had more debt outstanding than others, and some had been more responsible about retiring their debt than others. Hamilton said before the Constitution that all state debts were essentially the same and their redemption would spread the burden of financing the war more fairly and evenly, and remove a major obstacle to restoring the financial integrity of the country. Better to start fresh with all debts consolidated and only one system of public credit in operation.

Another issue was whether the debt should be redeemed at par, i.e., at full face value, when it was trading in the market at big discounts from par. Why not make an offer to buy it back at, say, seventy-five cents on the dollar, an offer that would save a great deal of money and no doubt would be fully subscribed? Hamilton said that the government would lose credibility in financial markets everywhere if it were seen to be cheating its creditors out of full payment, a view supported by financial people, but they were not in the majority. Hamilton's task was not just to make the right decision about this, but also to sell it to a majority of the new members of Congress. The question of whether the treasury would or would not redeem this debt was contentious and fiercely debated, but ultimately the Congress adopted Hamilton's plan.

Hamilton, Jefferson, and Madison traded support for Hamilton's debt plan by agreeing to the location of the future capital city along the Potomac River, an issue of great importance to southern congressmen. The debt assumption and redemption decision were the vital steps for the new country to take—steps that contributed more than any other to its quickly built reputation for fiscal responsibility and for honoring its credit standing in financial markets.

The assumption of the debt finally cost the new American government close to $65 million, including arrearages. This was about 15 percent of the estimated market value of all the land in all the states, therefore a considerable amount. It was estimated that the speculators of the time, the earliest of our bond-market arbitrage players to be "bailed-out" by the government, received about $40 million of that. Hamilton, a practical man, was well aware of the purchases of outstanding debt at deep discounts from the original holders, but he believed that the trade-off was necessary and worthwhile. And it was. But it was also a highly courageous political act to take early in the days of the new republic, when the common people of the country—well accustomed to gathering in dangerous, unruly mobs—were waiting to see whether they could trust the new American system.

In considering the problems of national credit, Hamilton had more than a little help from a lengthy chapter in *The Wealth of Nations*. "Money . . . and the Expense of Maintaining the National Capital." Adam Smith did not have much to work with in preparing his very perceptive analysis of the theory of money and banking—the British banking system was still undeveloped when he wrote in the 1770s—but his ideas would have been useful to America's first treasury secretary. Smith offers a description of both fixed and circulating capital and their importance in an economic system, explains how the expandability of the monetary system depends on credit and credibility (and some worthwhile expense of maintaining the system), and shows how a banking system based on paper money and the sensible use of bank reserves can leverage the availability of capital within an economy. Not much of this was generally known in North America, where the British had not allowed banks and the experience of most merchants and planters had been with banks or factors located in London.

Hamiliton was well aware that future economic development depended heavily on the ability to attract and use capital efficiently, and he must have been interested in Adam Smith's essay on the way money and banking had been developed in Scotland. That country was poor and quite undeveloped economically when it joined the British union in 1707; it had only a small amount of money in circulation, which had to be turned in (and counted) for recoining. Starting around 1750, Smith said, banking operations had begun in Scotland:

". . . by the erection of new banking companies in almost every considerable town . . . the business of the country is almost entirely carried on by means of the paper of those different banking companies, with which purchases and payments of all kinds are commonly made . . . I have heard it asserted that the trade in the city of Glasgow doubled in about fifteen years after the first erection of banks there, and that the trade of Scotland has more than quadrupled since the first banks were opened in Edinburgh (one in 1697, the other in 1727)."

This being the case, banking may have been more developed in Scotland in Adam Smith's time than it was in England, where we can rely on Toynbee's description of a weak banking system.

Under Hamilton's direction, debt assumption, a new currency, a tax-collection system, and the formation of a central bank that stabilized and fortified American finances were in place by 1795. Europe was plunged into the Napoleonic wars by then, and many wealthy Europeans were looking for a safe place to put their money. Because of its quick rise to financial respectability, the United States was seen as such a haven. Foreign holdings of American public debt increased from $2.7 million in 1788 to $5.7 million by 1790, and then to more than $20 million in 1795 from purchases at par or higher. Foreigners also purchased 13,000 of the 25,000 shares of stock in the new Bank of the United States, issued in 1798. Other new banks opened and there were more than twenty by 1800. "Our public credit," a jubilant President Washington wrote as early as July 1791, "stands on that ground, which three years ago it would have been considered a species of madness to have foretold."[10] The financial system became credible and markets opened to it—a development that many countries have since learned is much easier to prescribe than to achieve.

Hamilton and his early Federalist government colleagues were responsible for the formation of many of the country's most important public institutions: the systems of federal taxation, of government finance, of public credit and banking, and of the currency itself. All these labors of public office to create an effective, integrated system of public finance certainly merit the country's gratitude. But Hamilton did more than that. He also breathed the force of life into the private sector. He was the author of the government's *Report on Manufactures,* which advocated subsidies for a variety of activities that would encourage industrial manufacturing to provide a route to economic development other than traditional dependence on agriculture. It was also a blueprint for much of his subsequent advocacy for a strong federal government at the heart of all things economic. The report was not adopted as Hamilton proposed it, but it greatly influenced the public debate and developed many supporters. He urged a policy of tariff protection and subsidies that would force domestic industries into being and shelter them until they were strong enough to compete in world trade circles. Congress passed tariff laws in 1789, and again in 1792, that approved eighteen of his twenty-one recommended increases and three of his five reductions. By 1800, nearly a million tons of new shipping was in construction.

But perhaps the most important contribution to the development of the private sector of business and finance was the assurance that the public sector was efficient and confidence-inspiring. Without this, the banking system and securities markets could not have developed as they did. Without these institutions functioning well, development in the private sector as a whole would be constrained. The real economic development of the country was occasioned through the private business and financial sectors, not the government sector, but the former could not function effectively if the latter did not. America's first decade of financial institution-building may have provided one of the country's highest return on investments ever achieved.[11]

EARLY AMERICAN ENTERPRISE

Robert Morris was the leading financial figure during the revolutionary war, and the Confederation period. He was appointed superintendent of finance of the Continental Congress in 1781 and held the position until 1784, after which a "Board of the Treasury" dealt with public finance until the new Treasury Department, under Hamilton, came on stream in 1789. Morris served as an apprentice to a wealthy Philadelphia merchant whose son, at the death of his father, took Morris into partnership. In 1765, while active in opposition to the Stamp Tax, Morris married an attractive, wealthy woman and moved into one of Philadelphia's finest homes. His firm, Willing & Morris, was rated among the largest and most prosperous of the American commercial houses at the time of the Revolution. A strong supporter of the break with Britain, Morris was elected to the Continental Congress in 1775, and was a signer of the Declaration of Independence. As a financial man, he was assigned to those committees of Congress that dealt with war finance. In 1779, he funded Nathanael Greene's southern campaigns, and the next year raised $1.4 million for Washington's march to Yorktown. As superintendent of finance, he was responsible for budgets, purchases, and accounting under the Articles of Confederation and was constantly attempting to persuade the states to fulfill the agreed-upon quotas for money, credit, and supplies.

In December 1781, the financial situation of the Confederation had become desperate and the government was $2.5 million in debt. Morris met the occasion by organizing the Bank of North America, the country's first financial institution to be incorporated by Congress, and it opened its doors for business in January 1782, with capital of $400,000.

Morris was also a member of the Constitutional Convention and signed the Constitution for Pennsylvania. From 1789 to 1795, he served as U.S. senator from Pennsylvania. Offered the post of treasury secretary in the new government by Washington, he declined, recommending

Hamilton instead. After the war, he went into business, trading in the East Indies and China and speculating heavily in land through the North American Land Company. Both of these businesses, formerly prohibited by the British, were extremely appealing to Morris, who raised a lot of money for them on his personal credit. When the bottom fell out of the land businesses in 1795, Morris was unable to meet his debts and was imprisoned from February 1795 until liberated by the passage of the national bankruptcy laws in 1802.

Similarly, Henry Lee, a war hero known as "Light Horse Harry," sought to turn his self-confidence, energy, and zeal to building a fortune in the new country. Lee was a fifth-generation Virginian, a wealthy man and substantial landowner, born and raised at Stratford Hall near the Potomac, where his son, Robert E. Lee, was born in 1807. His family was very distinguished—two uncles had signed the Declaration of Independence, two others were prominent diplomats, and another a judge. Harry Lee had served in the Continental Light Dragoons under Generals Washington and Greene, and won a gold medal from Congress for his actions in combat.

After the war, Lee believed that the new system of government without the hated British would open the door to great money-making opportunities. He believed, as did many Americans at the time, that western land was the key to wealth, and he bought extensive holdings of undeveloped land in Virginia, North Carolina, Kentucky, Pennsylvania, and Georgia. This land was to be resold to the wave of settlers that was certain to cross the Allegheny Mountains, and to wealthy foreign investors who, he believed, would pour into the country now that its independence had been recognized and peace secured. In addition, Lee was fascinated by a scheme first promoted before the war by George Washington and some others to build a canal around the Great Falls of the Potomac River. This would open the river above the falls to navigation, but the British had disallowed the project. The Potomac Company was incorporated after the war and raised money by selling stock to build the canal and charge tolls for using it. (Canals had been built throughout England to improve local transportation starting in the mid-eighteenth century, and were very successful.) The Potomac canal would be the first to be built in America expressly for the purpose of opening western trade with the eastern seaboard. (The Erie Canal was begun in 1817.)

Tobias Lear, a secretary to George Washington and familiar with the Potomac project, said that knowledgeable and conservative men who had reviewed it "had no doubt as to [the canal's] producing 50-percent [return on capital] annually in less than ten years from the tolls."[12] Further, with a canal in place, commercial traffic between the western regions and the open sea could come down the Potomac, creating a rise in local land prices. Lee was convinced, and he bought shares in the canal, as well as 500 acres of land for the development of a new city to be located near Alexandria, Virginia, and 200,000 acres upriver, which he hoped to resell for three times his investment within five years. Lee also loaned $40,000 to Robert Morris to join his efforts.

However, the demand for backcountry land never moved beyond the small settlers, who appeared as expected but who had little money. The important European investors proved to be hesitant, and they were able to find high returns from loans to governments involved in the Napoleonic wars, which were then just beginning. Also, it turned out that trade from the Ohio River would have to go through other canals to reach the upper Potomac, and these canals were, unfortunately, never built. In 1795, land values turned downward, and by 1797, much of the credit extended for land purchases was in default. The Potomac canal was abandoned, and Lee's creditors closed in. He was ruined financially and went to jail for nonpayment of his debts in 1809.

Morris and Lee were both high-stakes players, betting heavily on their vision of the new American future, which they believed would most likely be revealed in rising land prices, the ancient standard of value. Both were high-ranking, well-connected Americans in 1790, but they miscalculated. Western migration did not develop as rapidly as they had thought it would, and, overextended, both died broke. But others entered the commercial arena at around the same time and did much better. Some were recent immigrants, coming from families of no social position and no money but arriving with lots of energy and ambition. Some of them were very successful.

Steven Girard became the wealthiest American in the new United States at the turn of the nineteenth century. He was one of five children of a French sea captain—he went to sea himself, beginning as a cabin boy, and commanded a trading vessel by the age of twenty-three. After the Revolution had begun, his ship was fogbound in the Delaware River. He learned that the British were blockading offshore, so he proceeded upriver to Philadelphia, where he sold the vessel and its cargo (which he did not own) and set up in the grocery business. He became an unscrupulous, if opportunistic, trader—dealing illegally with the British on one day, running the British blockade on another, and slave-trading on the next. He financed privateers, smuggling, and other shady operations tolerated by wartime conditions. At the end of the war, Girard expanded his business into a fleet of eighteen ships, which sailed the U.S.-Europe-Caribbean routes that the British had made difficult for American shipping. In 1812, at the outbreak of war, he suddenly converted his shipping fortune into banking. When Congress did not renew the twenty-year charter of the first Bank of the United States, the bank had to close. Girard, who had been the largest investor, bought the building and opened his own bank, the Girard

Bank. During the War of 1812, he was one of a small group of wealthy men who financed the U.S. Government. Described as an ugly old skinflint with no family of his own, he was possibly the model for Scrooge in Charles Dickens's *Christmas Carol*. Like Scrooge, he had a late-in-life conversion and bestowed large gifts to charities all over Philadelphia. His wealth was estimated at $7.5 million at the time of his death in 1831.

John Jacob Astor came to America after the Revolution, from the town of Waldorf in the Black Forest region of Germany. He was the son of a butcher and the brother of a flute-maker. He landed in New York with a handful of flutes, which he sold, then began working for a furrier, having heard tales of riches in the fur trade on his passage. There was a powerful demand in Europe for fine beaver skins, from which to make men's top hats. Soon he began his own business, the American Fur Company. However, Canadians then controlled the fur trade. Nevertheless, Astor trudged up the Mohawk Valley establishing trading posts with the Indian tribes that gathered most of the pelts. He offered them whiskey and other incentives to persuade them to sell their pelts to him. By 1793, he was shipping over 100,000 beaver pelts to Europe each year and managing his costs carefully. He plunged into the new opportunities in fur trading occasioned by the Louisiana Purchase and became the fur king of the world. Then, after thirty years, he sold it all, switching his interest to New York

City real estate at just the right time. The fur trade declined as interest in beaver-skin top hats waned, while land prices in Manhattan were rising fast. John Jacob Astor died in 1848, leaving a fortune of $20 to $25 million, the largest in the country at the time. His son William became the "Landlord of New York," owning at the time of his death in 1875 more than seven hundred buildings and houses in the city, many of them slums.

In 1789, Samuel Slater left Derbyshire for America, carrying in his head plans for Richard Arkwright's steam-powered, automated mill for spinning yarn. Slater, who had a natural aptitude for mechanics, was in the right place at the right time. He had apprenticed in a stocking factory and was one of the key factory workers at the mill cele-brated for its contribution to the English Industrial Revolu-tion. He had thought to set up his own business in England, but there was too much competition. The new technology had spread rapidly, and there were by then hundreds of tex-tile mills. So Slater thought he would answer an advertise-ment placed by the Pennsylvania legislature offering a bounty to experienced textile workers who came to the United States. The trouble was that Britain so prized its leadership in the textile industry that it was illegal for machinery or plans to be exported. It was even a crime, punishable with imprisonment, for experienced textile workers to try to leave the country. Still, the bounty was offered and Slater meant to have it. He smuggled himself out of the country to New York, where he made contact with Moses Brown, a wealthy Quaker merchant who wanted to build an Arkwright mill in Rhode Island. Slater hired on, built the mill a year later (1790), and helped to establish the New England textile industry, one of the country's most lucrative industries, for more than a hundred years.[13] Slater later branched out on his own and became a prominent manufacturer himself. He died in 1835 with a fortune of over a million dollars.

The new United States of America was rapidly becoming a land of opportunity. There was no trace of European feudalism—no nobility with special privileges, no system of "influence" to determine one's success, no practice of allocating valuable government properties and licenses to favored supporters of the Crown. Instead, an extraordinary new system of equal access and opportunity was burgeoning in a land of great resources with much work to be done. Adam Smith's notion of the linkage between common justice, self-interest, and economic progress was being vindicated in the new American nation. Girard and Astor could rise from their low origins. Morris and Lee could fail despite their high positions. Slater's self-interest would spur him to move to a better market. So also being indicated were Adam Smith's conjoined ideas about the role of government in an economic society designed to maximize opulence—first, that government involvement in the allocation of resources and subsidies should be replaced by the action of free markets, and second, that government should concentrate its efforts toward providing public institutions (banks) and infrastructure (canals and roads), and assuring national defense. The American experience was to become a golden opportunity for the principal theories of Adam Smith to be tested. And the new Americans, eager to have all useful advice that would help them build a new political-economic system that would survive, found Smith's ideas both applicable and practical.

In time, a hundred years or so according to Adam Smith, the American economic system would rise to surpass even that of the mighty British Empire. But not unless the Revolution had occurred would Smith's ideas and theories be so clearly put to the test. And not unless the new country survived would his theories appear to mean anything.

CHAPTER 4

———◆◆◆———

HARDENING THE TEMPLATE

By 1800, the new American republic had survived some of its most perilous years, and much of its Adam Smith–inspired template of a political economy based on democratically operated free markets had been realized, at least on a tentative basis. Survival, of course, was the real goal, and to survive, most of the founders knew that the new political economy of the United States would have to be successful in generating opulence. Adam Smith had now been dead for a decade, his recommendations for policies to improve the economy still ignored in Britain. A revolution in France had erupted in violence and chaos, and the predicted tyrant, Napoleon, had appeared and plunged all Europe into war. America was out of sight to Europeans at this time, and its weaknesses did not attract any predators. The country was largely left to develop itself, if it could, without falling back on the old ways of Europe. The nation had chosen its template during the first Washington administration and was making every effort to harden it up so it could last. But there were still many challenges ahead.

Washington's eight years in office had established at least three important legacies: credibility for the federal system; confidence in the democratic ideals of the Constitution, particularly when Washington retired from office after serving only two terms; and the enduring foundations of the American economic system. However, it would not take much, many people worried at the time, to throw the new United States of America off its base precipitating the whole costly experiment into failure.

John Adams became President in 1796 and never had a day without feeling the danger. The effects of the French Revolution were boiling over in America. There was sympathy for the new Directoire (the ever-shifting cabal leading the French after their revolution began) on the part of Thomas Jefferson and his political allies, who seemed somehow able to reconcile the cherished spirit of liberty, equality, and fraternity with the murder and bloodshed that followed. There were then approximately 25,000 French émigrés living in America—some who had remained behind after the war, some who were refugees from the Terror, or the slave uprisings in the Caribbean, and some who were agents sent to America to stir up trouble, which they did. The French Directoire had little regard for the American success in overthrowing a king and establishing a republic; mainly, it perceived America as a weak country on which it could prey. The Directoire had issued orders for the raiding of American shipping, and by 1798, it had seized an estimated three hundred trading vessels and injured (even tortured) American seamen.[1]

Then news was released that senior French officials (the so-called Messrs. "X," "Y," and "Z") had asked for payment (bribes) from the American government to normalize relations. Americans were outraged and wanted to strike out at the French, but they were opposed by the Directoire's Republican supporters (such as Jefferson) and by the Adams government, which felt that the new country was completely unready to battle another large country. There was no clear information about events—everything people were told was subject to distortion and unverified rumors, including word that the French had declared war on the United States and were planning an invasion of Florida and the Mississippi Delta. Riots and other disturbances broke out in Philadelphia as the country began to prepare itself for war with France. Adams did spend some federal money on building a navy—the first government intervention in the economy for the purpose of national defense—and agreed to a few other preparations, but he did everything he could to avoid having to declare war, for fear of losing it. He also signed the Alien and Sedition Acts, which he regarded as "war measures" to better control the turbulent conditions in the country. These controversial Acts, however, were seen to impinge on basic American democratic freedoms and to undermine the Revolution, and Adams could not survive his association with them.

In 1800, Thomas Jefferson was elected to succeed Adams, and Napoleon Bonaparte seized power in France. Bonaparte hoped to recover all French interests in America. He sent an armed force to the Caribbean to do so and dispatched troops from France to crush a slave revolt in Santo Domingo. However, ferocious resistance and yellow fever wiped out the army. Finally, frustrated and distracted by more pressing matters in Europe, Napoleon decided instead to sell the Louisiana Territory—800,000 square miles west of the Mississippi—to the United States for $15 million in 1803. The deal again doubled the size of the land area of the United States, which had already doubled once at the conclusion of the revolutionary war. The purchase also dispelled growing fears of war with the French and allowed American politics to return to normal. The country was now overwhelmed with undeveloped, unsettled land, from the Alleghenies to the Rocky Mountains, containing vast amounts of natural resources.

Thomas Jefferson's writing and political activities have established him as an "anti-Federalist," one who preferred greater allocation of power to the states and a return to the "simpler state of an agricultural society." Though he always disclaimed interest in party politics, he became the center of opposition to the Federalist party and allowed a "Republican" party (now the modern Democrats) to form around him. The central platform of the Federalist party (later the modern Republicans) was the support of strong central government and the development of a strong urban economy based on trade, manufactures, and banking. Its opponents believed that these policies would lead to "monarchial" practices and ambitions. The Republicans endorsed an opposite set of policies: a weak federal government, strict limitation of the application of constitutional powers, and an economic system based on land development and easy credit to farmers. Federalists believed that such policies would lead to a return to an impotent government such as that under the Articles of Confederation. These distinctions were sharpened for propaganda purposes as each side endeavored to gain support from the masses of common people, whose power was feared in mob actions more than at the ballot box.

However, the fact is that the two parties' attitudes about economic development were about the same. When Jefferson became President in 1801, he and his protégés, Madison and Monroe, who made up the tight Virginian-Republican cohort, began a span of control of the top executive office that lasted for twenty-four years. During this time, none of

Hamilton's original economic measures were dissolved. Protective tariffs were continued. The charter of the Bank of the United States was renewed. And the Louisiana Purchase (a wide departure from the "strict construction" policies of the Constitution, so ardently favored by Jefferson), was justified as offering a possible navigable northwest passage across North America to the Pacific, which it did not, and a means to dominate the lucrative fur trade, which it did.

Jefferson believed that as President, he could not convert the entire country to his ways of thinking about economic priorities, and instead, he decided to go with the flow and let people decide for themselves. He knew that whatever their experience over the past decade, the people ultimately wanted economic opportunity, which could not be gained if frustrated by abstract principles and ideals. They wanted land (and people to work it), roads and related public infrastructure, financial services, and modern industry. He never opposed these demands, nor did he ever think it important or necessary to do so.

Jefferson had an extraordinary finance chief, Albert Gallatin, who served for twelve years in both Jefferson's and Madison's administrations. Gallatin, like Hamilton, was born abroad, was orphaned early in life, immigrated to the United States as a young man, and excelled on arrival. Before taking up the treasury at the age of forty (Hamilton was thirty-nine), Gallatin had been a member of the Con-

stitutional Convention and of the Pennsylvania state legislature. He became a passionate Republican and was one of
Jefferson's most partisan supporters. He was elected to the
senate from Pennsylvania (but the Federalists refused to
seat him because, they said, he had not been a citizen long
enough to hold a seat), and later served as an influential
member of the House of Representatives (which let him
in). Like Hamilton, he supported a strong central bank, and
he prepared a report on manufactures in which he featured
high tariffs on manufactured imports. Gallatin also had a
controlling mission, that of developing a democratic,
broadly expanding internal economy. He was tough on
government expenditures and fostered reduction of the
national debt despite the war with the Barbary pirates and
the Louisiana Purchase, mainly by cutting back on military
investments initiated by Adams. Only here did he depart
from Hamilton's (and Adam Smith's) principal policies
that advocated a strong national defense. Gallatin supported Jefferson's opinion that defense was a lesser priority than building up the economy. In 1808, upon leaving
office, Jefferson noted that because of—

". . . increasing application of our industry and capital
to internal manufactures and improvements . . . little
doubt remains that the establishments formed and
forming—under the auspices of cheaper materials and

subsistence, the freedom of labor from taxation with us, and of protecting duties and prohibitions—*will become permanent*."[2] (Emphasis added.)

Madison's administration was largely focused on the events leading to the War of 1812 and its prosecution (and financing). The war officially ended in 1817, and Monroe was able to shift his sights to foreign affairs, obtaining Florida from Spain, settling the Canadian border, and pronouncing his doctrine to warn off European adventures in any part of the Americas. John Quincy Adams was next as President for one term. Andrew Jackson, the victor at the Battle of New Orleans, succeeded him in 1829. Jackson, the great populist, continued to support the tariff policies of his predecessors, but he was determined to defeat the charter renewal of the Bank of the United States, which he did, leaving the country without a central bank for more than eighty years. Jackson's secretary of the treasury during the war against the Bank of the United States was Roger Taney, who became chief justice of the U.S. Supreme Court in 1836. In one of his first opinions as chief justice, Taney made it clear that the Constitution restricted the power of the state to grant special privileges to any corporate group except for promotion of the public interest.[3] Put another way, Taney was warning business leaders that they could bribe legislators or others to pass laws that conveyed special benefits for themselves, but these laws could be overturned by the judicial system. This ruling left legislative corruption in the hands of the courts, rather than leaving the legislatures to regulate themselves, unlike prevailing practices in Europe.

Martin Van Buren succeeded Jackson, but the "crash of 1837," which led to a five-year depression, ended his hopes for a second term. William Henry Harrison, an Indian war hero, died shortly after his inauguration and was succeeded by an unknown John Tyler, who served only one term and remains unknown. In 1845, James K. Polk, another one-term President was elected, and he made a big difference on the country's future by prosecuting the Mexican War of 1846 that ended with the annexation of California and the southwestern territories, and by deciding the northwestern borders of the United States. Polk's land grabs almost doubled the size of the United States yet again, and finally fixed its continental boundaries, ending the rolling-frontier period of American history. By then, too, the general free-market template had been settled in place by familiarity and usage, by success in its application, and by the political satisfactions that rising prosperity in America was able to bestow on an increasingly democratic political system.

AMERICAN ECONOMIC STRATEGIES

In the early years of the new republic, there must have been debates over differing strategies for economic development beyond the simplistic notions that Hamilton favored manufactures and Jefferson favored agriculture. The founders wanted their political ideals to succeed, but for this to occur, the country first had to become economically stable. It would be natural enough, therefore, for Hamilton and the others to copy the most successful economic elements of the most successful countries they were aware of, those that had long since become rich and powerful. If they were to have picked one country as a model, it would have been Britain, its former parent, which had gained so much wealth and influence for a small island country and to which America remained connected by language and heritage. Hamilton in particular wanted to rebuild the economic bridge to Britain. He was aware, through Adam Smith's writings, that Britain's opulence came partly from the agricultural dominance of the domestic economy and partly from the mercantile system by which its colonial trade was run.

Land, according to Smith, represented value because it gainfully employed labor to provide sustenance and produced raw materials that could be sold or processed into trade goods. To be efficient, however, landholdings had to be large enough that economies of scale could be achieved.

Such large landholdings were established in the first place by grants from central authority (the Crown, in the case of Britain) and added to by purchase and marriage. To work their land, the owners employed local farmers as tenants, maintaining full civil and economic power over them. To preserve the landholdings, laws of primogeniture and entail existed in order to pass entire estates to the oldest surviving sons. Landholdings also entailed political power through control of nominees from their districts, and this power, combined with that of other landowners, was usually sufficient to protect agricultural interests against adverse legislation.

The system had worked well (it was thought) for more than a thousand years; it was understood and accepted by all Europeans. It was the survivor of an ancient feudal system that was hardly democratic or republican, but many Americans owned the land they did because of the application of the European system to the American colonies by the British.

After 1803, America had an almost inconceivable amount of land to be distributed for development. It would not have been difficult to allow state governors or federal officials to perform the task by selling or granting land to rich individuals, those most likely to afford the investments necessary for its development. Certainly, many of America's founding fathers were rich enough and sufficiently well connected to include themselves in the largesse, a tradition that eighteenth-century society would have expected and tolerated. But it was not to be. Americans had ingested too much democracy for such a scheme to be approved in a public forum. Many Americans believed that the worst of British arrogance and oppression derived from its practice of sustaining a landed aristocracy. In any case, the general population was still out there, as potentially dangerous as ever to a constitutional democracy, and it wanted access to the land, too.

Meanwhile, a favorable trade balance, most people believed, would provide access to cash and opulence. This was the other part of the British model that emphasized agriculture at home together with an aggressive mercantile trade with an expanding group of compliant colonies. In Europe, colonies were seen as repositories of low-cost natural raw materials (sugar, spices, tobacco, cotton) that could be exploited while they lasted and then replaced. Americans appreciated cash and opulence, too, and might well have gone off in search of colonies of their own. The British, French, Spanish, and Dutch all prospered from colonial trade. Indeed, Britain, which emerged as the European superpower after the Battle of Waterloo that ended the Napoleonic era, spent the rest of the century exploring and further colonizing the world, until it controlled about 25 percent of it. If colonies were so important to national wealth, shouldn't America have some too, at least while there were still some available?

The Americans probably could have found colonial opportunities in the Caribbean (e.g., Cuba, Haiti, the Dutch islands), Central America (Mexico), and South America (Brazil, Peru), possibly even in Canada. This might have been feasible during the twenty or thirty unstable years from the French Revolution in 1789 until the wars of liberation fought by the South Americans against Spain after 1820. By this time, but certainly after the Mexican War in 1848, America would have been able to assemble an adequate military force to do as it wanted in the region.

Also, by 1840, the Negro slave population had swollen to several million and was now almost entirely utilized in the production of cotton. Arguably, this enclave of slavery was a colony within the greater American economic system. But there is no evidence that the idea of acquiring colonies outside the internal American market, including those that might have expanded the American experience with slavery, was ever considered seriously. There were negatives in doing so. Adam Smith pointed out that colonies required military force to secure and defend, were unstable, changeable, and often difficult and expensive to govern. Accordingly, the mercantile system was not economically reliable, because colonies wore out or changed hands too often and too easily.

So neither the establishment of a landed gentry nor a policy of colonial acquisition was adopted in the United States, despite valid precedents to do so. Both policies were of course out of fashion after twenty-five years of American political rhetoric and would not have been acceptable to the American electorate. Also, Adam Smith had claimed that both would impair free markets, prevent a just distribution of economic resources in society, and preclude self-interest from emerging as a major motivating force for economic development. Colonies detracted from economic efficiency, Smith said, more than they added to it. Smith's writings on these subjects may not have been widely read in the United States, but many of the founding fathers knew of them, as did many of the more learned statesmen who followed.

But arguably, America was untempted by the old models because it had something entirely different to work with—the vast quantities of unsettled land to the west and a shortage of people to settle it. This was a development opportunity that no other nation had experienced and was completely alien to conditions in post-feudal Europe. Settling this land and making it part of the active, expanding economy became *the* national priority. This priority accounted for the great flows of immigration that began after the War of 1812, and the constant requirement that American society adapt to new people, places, ideas, and opportunities.

But the priority given to land settlement had to be backed up by sound and credible land-ownership policies or it would begin to appear to be unachievable and not attract the requisite immigration. What made it work was the absence of government involvement in protecting landed interests—there were no laws or policies (such as existed in Europe) that either favored the rich or suppressed the smaller farmers and laborers. During the bulk of the nineteenth century, America was able to attract constant immigration of both people and capital to its open, free-trading marketplace. The country filled with immigrants looking for land and opportunity, which were continuously made available by the westward expansion. This movement developed considerable political support, and America's "Manifest Destiny" to own and occupy all the land on the continent from "sea to shining sea" was widely encouraged.

In his first annual message to Congress as President, Thomas Jefferson stated: "Agriculture, manufactures, commerce and navigation, the four pillars of our prosperity, are the most thriving when left most free to individual enterprise." This laissez-faire viewpoint sounds more like Adam Smith's policies than Jefferson's, but Jefferson's policies were not just his own. As President, he understood that he had to be practical and use strategies that worked. And what worked were the original fiscal policies set forth by Hamilton and followed by all his successors. Indeed, as Jefferson observed, these initial policies of free markets and fiscal responsibility had firmly taken root and "become permanent" in the country.

FOUR PILLARS OF AMERICAN ENTERPRISE

The four main pillars of the American economy that Jefferson pointed to in 1804 developed during the nineteenth century into many more complex and interrelated components. But the pillars he identified in the early days of the century were still the most important even at the end of the nineteenth century.

- Agriculture. For at least a hundred years after 1800, the former North American colonies had a large surplus of land that was made available to land-hungry farmers from the eastern states and Europe. As in colonial days, the land had to be cleared and settled to have any value, and the value would accrue to those willing to claim ownership and do the work themselves. But it was not quite so simple. The government now owned the land and had to set up rules for its distribution. Large tracts were offered to developers who could find settlers to buy it. The settlers were a diverse group, but they did have one thing in common—they saw the self-interested opportunity to better themselves and acted on it. Once having bought the land, settlers had to clear it, live on it, defend it against Indians, outlaws and land-grabbers, and the ravages of weather and climate. They had to know how to cope and to be willing to do so for long, lonely periods of time. It was not for everyone, but it appealed to those with a high tolerance for risk and to those with nothing to lose. The challenges were daunting, and many failed in the effort or died trying.

The lure of the land drew these people away from ordinary jobs in the East and wages there rose accordingly, further attracting immigrants from Europe, where overcrowded countries had forced wages to the bottom (a mechanism described by Adam Smith). Ownership of land held a great appeal to almost all the immigrants, but they were realistic and knew it would take time to buy it, even in America where uncleared land was cheap. In the meantime, they would have to find what work they could. The individuals that came were looking to rise above the miserable living conditions they had left, or hoping, like Samuel Slater, to sell their valuable skills for a profit. This infused the country with millions of courageous, energetic, and ambitious new citizens and their future children, all of whom were lost to the overcrowded, oppressive Old World labor markets of Europe. In 1850, the total population of the United States was about 25 million, of which 2.2 million were foreign-born and many more were children of first-generation immigrants. Of the 2.2 million, 66 percent were of British origin, including more than half who were Irish. Indeed, hard-pressed Irish immigrants, chafing in poverty under British rule they could not throw off, were vastly more numerous after 1820 than those from all the rest of the British Empire combined. By 1900, the American population contained 10.3 million foreign-born, of which about 35 percent were British. In all, Winston Churchill claimed in his *History of the English Speaking Peoples*, more than 8 million Britons left the country for America, carrying British traditions and culture with them, while easing the unfortunate pressure of overcrowding in the country whose own Industrial Revolution could not fully absorb them.

In fact, economic life in Britain was becoming even harsher for those lacking privileges. In England, Scotland, and Wales, land was being enclosed and penniless tenants evicted in favor of a growing sheep industry. Industrialization led to exploitative working conditions in factories and mines; urban poverty was extensive and criminal penalties severe. The cautious ones stayed at home hoping for the best, while the brave and the bold (if also the poor and the desperate) were those who came to America. It was a good trade for America, as it got the plucky ones that it needed. More than 20 million immigrants settled in America between 1820 and 1900, and this flight further encouraged those who would invest their capital in the country, too.

Western migration was accelerated by two other factors. One was a gold rush in California following its annexation from Mexico in 1849; the search for gold and other metals in the western states and Alaska continued for many years. The gold fever itself attracted thousands out of their eastern livelihoods and brought them west, where many would remain. The other factor was the effort by the federal government to lure European settlers by offering free and bonus land to those who would live on it (the last "land rush" was in Oklahoma in 1893) and by the establishment of federal land-grant colleges, which offered higher education to rural settlers. In the 1850s, railroads were also advertising for settlers. The town of Bismarck, North Dakota, was so named in 1872 by land developers of the Northern Pacific Railroad to attract sturdy, reliable farmers from Germany and Scandinavia to move there, which many did. These settlers were among the first American entrepreneurs— risking all on an outcome sustained by hard work, determination, and luck. They certainly set the example for those who followed them.

Even with the western settlers in place, however, land development presented other problems. The Indians, periodically hostile, had to be pushed west methodically, and were brutally dispatched when they got in the way. As settlers moved west, they had to be accompanied by army troops to protect them, and some sort of law and order had to find its way into the frontier regions. But a greater problem was the potential impact of slavery on the settlement of the West. Slavery was already a divisive issue in American politics. In 1808, federal law prohibited the importation of slaves, though smuggling continued and there were still millions of slaves in bondage in the country. In 1820, a generally unsatisfactory Missouri Compromise was brokered in which slavery was permitted in Missouri but not elsewhere west of the Mississippi or north of the southern border of Missouri. By then, slavery had become unprofitable in large parts of the South, though it took some time for all the southerners to realize it. As tobacco crops were less in demand, so was slavery in Virginia and North Carolina. Many of those slaves were sold farther south (and then west) to the cotton fields, where there was great need for labor. Cotton had become the great cash crop of the South after the Revolution, and planters had huge demand for it from newly industrialized cotton-mill operators in New England and Britain. Some owners may have thought of taking their slaves and moving west with the wagon trains, but slavery was worthwhile only in the intensive production of cash crops with a ready market. Not many of those conditions applied in most parts of the land to be settled, though they did in a few, and slavery migrated as much as it was permitted to.

In much of the South, slavery contributed to an economic malaise and a period of low economic growth and development. A reluctance to give up the social elevation permitted by slavery, and the lack of need to participate in manual labor, separated many southerners from their northern counterparts. Racial prejudice killed initiative and turned isolated, rural southern planters and their white neighbors into defenders of the long-time status quo. There was very little manufacturing in the South; the cotton was shipped elsewhere to be spun and woven into cloth. Even in the antebellum period of the South, planters there were as dependent on "outsiders" for their livelihood as they were in colonial times. Southern labor mobility was low, and education among whites was inferior to that offered widely in the North. In general, from about 1820 until the beginning of the Civil War in 1861, economic growth in the South lagged behind that of all other American regions (the Northeast, the Middle Atlantic states, and the West).[4] After the war, it was even worse; cotton had passed on, and the wheat fields of the Midwest came to dominate American agriculture.

By the middle of the nineteenth century, the moral and humane objections to slavery were widely accepted, except in the South. The British had begun the practice of slavery in the colonial period in support of their mercantilist economic policies, which came to an end in 1776. As little as Adam Smith would wish to see mercantilism continued, he would have favored slavery even less. Slavery, from Smith's point of view, was an economic abomination—it suppressed the workers' pursuit of self-interest, imposed institutional restrictions on the mobility of labor, and discourage the ability of the market to set wage rates. It forcibly impressed labor, caused it to permanently endure in unjust circumstances, and imposed a heavy financial cost to enforce compliance with the system. It also extinguished the entrepreneurial environment, which had given rise to such rapid industrial development (and further self-improvement) in the northern states.

- Manufactures. Economists have argued for years over when in the nineteenth century the American economy reached the "take off" point leading to the high rate of per-capita economic growth that showed the effects of the Industrial Revolution. Because all agree that the available statistical data are virtually nonexistent, they have tried to back their way into a better understanding by using different approaches. Some have pointed to increases in trade, some to urbanization, improvement in transportation, and a lowered cost of commodities. Economists agree that industrialization in manufacturing began sometime after 1800. The steam engine was produced commercially in the U.S. in 1805, not long after it was first utilized in British industry in 1790. American cotton textile manufacturing was much advanced by industrial technologies developed in Britain; as were other industries that benefited from imitation. In 1807 (a year in which important protective tariff laws were enacted), the fifteen or twenty American cotton mills in existence employed about 8,000 spindles, but according to Gallatin's congressional report on manufactures, by 1811, it was expected that eighty-seven firms would be operating 80,000 spindles. By 1820, the spindle total had reached 190,000; by 1831, more than 1,250,00 spindles were in use and the manufacture of cotton textiles (much of it in enterprising New England) had become a substantial industry.

Similar growth figures appear for iron-making, woolen goods, carpets, paper, flint glass, lead, sugar, molasses, and salt. Gallatin's report to Congress in 1810 estimated that the annual production of manufactures had reached $120 million and that raw materials used in these efforts created a home market for them equal to that arising from foreign demand.[5] America was no longer just an exporter of raw materials—as were "third-world" countries and those trapped in a colonial mercantile system—but an important consumer, too. After 1820, urban population centers began to grow rapidly, and for new immigrants, jobs in manufacturing became an alternative to farming on the frontier and were a welcome supplemental source of income to their women and children.

As the home market for consumption of manufactures grew, more investment in technology could be justified, accelerating the rate of industrialization, which, in turn, needed more workers and more consumers to keep it going. In America, the immigration flow seemed endless, whereas the reverse was true in Britain. America was growing its own "customers" (an image and an idea that Adam Smith would have approved) while Britain had to replace its former American customers by turning to places such as India, China, and Africa. American tariffs, of course, excluded the most competitive British manufactures from the markets. These factors alone almost assured an American overtaking of British industrial output, though that did not occur until late in the nineteenth century.

- Commerce. When Jefferson identified "commerce" as one of the four pillars of the American economy, he probably meant retail and wholesale trade and the financial services to support them. The new urban populations were filling up with shopkeepers and distributors, and the less urban had the opportunity to deal with itinerant peddlers. Corporations were formed for the first time to undertake a variety of commercial ventures. The states chartered more than three hundred corporations between the Revolution and 1801. Because most of these early corporations were for transportation infrastructure, toll roads, bridges and canals, they had a quasi-public nature. Fire and marine insurance were particularly needed. So were water companies, dockyards, and other public utilities. Though they were still private-sector ventures, the federal and state governments often played a role. Subscriptions were made to raise money for stock issues, and sometimes governments would participate in them. In Pennsylvania, from 1790 to 1860, more than two thousand business corporations were chartered, of which 65 percent were in transportation, 11 percent in insurance, 7 percent each for general manufacturing and banking, and 3 percent each for gas, water, and miscellaneous categories. Corporations were perhaps more important in the picture than they appear, and they received a variety of government-supplied subsidies through tax abatement, tariff protection, and other rights or privileges.

Jefferson considered finance as part of the great commercial pillar. By finance, he would have meant the American banks and insurance companies created to provide essential services in support of domestic and international trade. Also included would have been a nationwide network of commercial banks needed to transact with the Bank of the United States for loans and deposits. Both proliferated during and after the Hamilton years and subsequently. In 1815, there were 208 state-chartered banks in operation with $45 million of bank notes outstanding. By 1860, the state-chartered banks had grown to 1,500, doing business with nearly $500 million of bank notes and deposits outstanding. In 1860, there were also 278 savings banks with deposits of $150 million.[6]

These banks were regulated only by state authorities, as the Bank of the United States had been put out of business in 1834. State banks were restricted to operating in and under the laws of the different states, and these laws varied. However, banking became something of a populist, highly transparent issue after Andrew Jackson's successful "war" to prevent renewal of the federal charter of the Bank of the United States, which he believed was an unnecessary monopoly and restricted free trade in banking. After Jackson's "victory," the American banking system settled into a rambling, disorganized, decentralized, state-by-state effort to lure funds from the conservative East for risky (but politically popular) loans to those on the western frontiers. The system certainly was not pretty, but it seemed to work, and there was no risk of monopoly concentrations in banking nationwide. The eastern bankers (largely "private banks" such as J. P. Morgan's) still controlled most of the investment capital and where it went, to the continuing irritation of the people in the West and their political representatives.

In addition to banking development, securities markets had emerged in New York and other regional centers. After about 1830, the New York Stock Exchange, founded by merchants in 1792, along with other regional stock exchanges, were actively trading government bonds, development bonds guaranteed by governments, the stocks and bonds of banks and the insurance companies, and railroad bonds. Less actively they also traded railroad stocks and a few industrial stocks for textile, mining, and gas-lighting companies. Boston was the center of the money markets until about 1850, when they moved permanently to New York.

Both state and federal governments were also active in providing financial aid to projects with great development potential. They did this through direct loans and by supporting the capital subscriptions of utilities, roadway and canal companies, and anything else they thought would advance their local development potential. And of course, the major source of investment capital for expanding companies was the reinvestment of their retained earnings, on which there were no income taxes until 1913.

The great American economic expansion of the nineteenth century was also due to the investment of large amounts of European capital made available by investors seeking high rates of return in this, the most promising "emerging market" of the day. Except for the Civil War period, the migration of money and workers was continuous during the nineteenth century. Investors preferred federal paper when they could get it (the national debt was, briefly, fully retired in 1836), then the obligations of state governments.

European capital was invested in American lands and enterprises from the earliest days of the republic. The process of gathering capital for investment was organized in the early 1800s, when representatives of distinguished European banking houses set up shop in New York, Philadelphia, and Boston. A wealthy young German banker, David Parish, came to the United States in 1805, where he was agent for Baring Brothers, the British merchant bank. He later surprised them by underwriting personally a third of a $16-million financing by the U.S. Government to pay for the War of 1812 against the British (Baring refused to participate in the loan).[7] In 1837, twenty-one-year-old German-born August Belmont, soon to become a prominent New York banker, became agent in the United States for the Rothschilds. Later, J. P. Morgan, representing his American father's London firm, also arranged investments in America for wealthy Europeans. Men such as these were attracted by the unique investment potential that America represented to the Old World, and by the opportunity to earn more than a 5 percent return, which seemed to be the norm for good-grade securities in London through most of the century. The total outstanding foreign indebtedness, public and private, of the United States in 1880 was $2.3 billion (up from $30 million in 1821). In 1868, the value of all securities traded in New York was about $3 billion.

Oxford economic historian D. C. M. Platt reminds us that the fledgling United States was indeed able to generate a substantial amount of domestic savings during the nineteenth century, when the annual average net national capital formation was 9.5 percent from 1834–1843, rising to 17.8 percent from 1869–1878. This was due to the strength and success of the institutions of finance—in both public and private sectors—that were established in the early days of the republic. Foreign capital, Platt suggests, never comprised much more than 6 percent of American requirements. However, it was the "gilt on the gingerbread," especially once the railroads appeared in the 1830s and 1840s. European investors were particularly attracted to railroad securities, judging them less risky and backed by substantial local interests. Platt estimated total foreign investment in U.S. railway securities between 1838 and 1878 to be $2.6 billion, of which approximately 90 percent were raised from British sources in London.[8]

- Navigation. Jefferson had internal water transportation as much in mind as he did ocean shipping when he named "navigation" as one of the key pillars of the economy. To develop the internal American market, an inexpensive way had to be found to ship goods from their point of production to the best markets for them. And in Jefferson's time, internal communications were primitive. Overland trails had been opened through the Allegheny Mountains to permit wagon travel into the Ohio Valley, but they were slow and expensive.

Robert Fulton successfully navigated his new steamboat, the *Clermont,* up the Hudson River in 1807. Upriver travel was very important, especially in the Mississippi region, which was developing into the cotton center of the world. Canals were attracting renewed interest, too, though the proposed Potomac canal was never realized. In 1817, authorization was secured in New York from the legislature to construct a canal linking the Great Lakes and the Mississippi to the Hudson River. The Erie Canal, which opened in 1825, was able within a few years to divert as much trade from the West as previously had descended the Mississippi to New Orleans, otherwise the only way to move goods out of the area. (Coming down the St. Lawrence was the only way to get them in.) The Erie Canal was one of the American wonders of the century—it lowered the cost of freight from Buffalo to New York twenty-fold. It gave great impetus to settling the West and enabled New York City to become the dominant commercial center of the country.

Railroads came next, another wonder of the century that managed to open new lands and permit long-distance commerce with settled markets all at once. The first railroad was laid down in Britain in 1825, and others were installed around the country throughout the century. The technology soon spread to America; its first railroad went down in 1830. In Britain, railways were useful to economic expansion; in America, they were essential. In 1868, the American railway system completed a transcontinental expansion covering more than three thousand miles, much of it over rugged, uninhabited terrain. Entire industries developed to support railroad expansion: mining, iron- and steel-making, the production of steam engines and railway cars, land development along rights-of-way, and the vital financial and legal services needed to keep the process going.

Meanwhile, of course, the real navigation—of ships at sea—also developed rapidly after the War of 1812. There were new trade routes to establish. Several hundred sturdy ships from numerous New England ports departed on two-year voyages to capture Pacific sperm whales and sell their oil to illuminate homes, a profitable industry that lasted for about fifty years before kerosene was marketed.

In the decade of 1846–1855, close to 250,000 ships were built in America, about three hundred of them the super-fast, sleek clipper ships that carried goods to China and back, around Cape Horn in record time.[9] Many of the most successful businessmen in America during the first half of the nineteenth century were men of "navigation." Most of them started as seamen, became captains, traded on behalf of their owners and themselves, became ship owners and owners of fleets. Many retired in their fifties and sat on the porches of their spacious New England waterfront houses that sprinkle the coastline today as upscale bed-and-breakfast hotels.

MID-CENTURY OPULENCE

Cornelius Vanderbilt, born in the eighteenth century, over-took John Jacob Astor as America's richest man when Astor died thirty years later with a fortune of over $100 million. Born on Staten Island of old but rustic Dutch stock, Vanderbilt started with little but became New York harbor's steamboat king. A large, foulmouthed and fiery individual of enormous energy, the "Commodore," as he called himself, ran barges, then ferries, then steamboats, then intercity liners, and a trans-Nicaraguan route to California during the gold rush. During the Civil War, he sold his oceangoing ships to the Navy, and nearing seventy, struck out in a new direction.

In 1862, he bought control of the New York and Harlem railroad, a small, unprofitable line that was the only railroad running into New York City, and began to improve it. He persuaded the aldermen of the city to approve an expansion of the line down to the Battery. He was opposed in this by his lifetime steamboat rival, the famously unscrupulous Daniel Drew, who attempted to bribe the aldermen into reversing their position. Vanderbilt persevered but spent most of the rest of his business career defending himself against such attacks, which were typical of the period. In 1864, he bought into the Hudson River Railroad, another small, unprofitable line that he wanted to connect to his Harlem line to create a single railroad from Albany to New York City. He needed permission of the legislature to do this, however, so he proceeded to get it. But Drew resurfaced and got the legislature to rescind the plan. Again, Vanderbilt prevailed, dealing a heavy blow to Drew and his supporters. Now he controlled the only line up the Hudson that connected to the New York Central lines heading to Chicago. During the winter months, the Central used this line to move its freight and passengers into and out of New York. During the rest of the year, however, the Central used one of Daniel Drew's steamboats to get to New York.

Vanderbilt did not like this arrangement, and he tried to negotiate with the Central line to change it, but without success. So in January of 1867, during a cold spell that had frozen the upper Hudson, he issued orders to his Hudson and Harlem line: "Take no more freight from the New York Central." That caused all traffic hauled by the Central to be stopped outside of Albany. This was a disaster for the Central, whose directors intervened, found their own managers responsible, and in a moment of unusual concern for shareholders' rights and good corporate governance, offered Vanderbilt control of the railroad. The New York Central then became a four-hundred-mile line stretching from the Great Lakes to New York City, at a time when the company's business and profits were about to expand greatly.

The following year, the Commodore was ready to acquire another line, the Erie, which ran up the Hudson on the western side of the river to Lake Erie and therefore also connected the New York area with the Midwest. Vanderbilt wanted to consolidate the Erie's business with the New York Central's and to eliminate overlaps. But the Erie was controlled by (guess who?) Daniel Drew. Having been bested by Vanderbilt in two earlier schemes, Drew decided to change tactics. He would encourage Vanderbilt to corner the Erie stock, then make it easy for him by printing new but unauthorized (and therefor illegal) stock certificates and selling these to him. Fellow Erie directors Jay Gould and Jim Fisk joined him in the plan and sold about $6 million of the phony shares, most of them to Vanderbilt. The Commodore got court intervention, but Drew and the others absconded with the money in carpetbags and holed up in a hotel in New Jersey. They stayed there for three months, protected by armed guards, until they could bribe the New York legislature to pass a law making all their actions legal. In the end, Drew and the others reached a settlement with Vanderbilt and the matter was closed.[10] For Vanderbilt, it may have been that the railroad business was not about trains but about stock market deals and battles, which he seemed to enjoy, and the stocks he acquired became extremely valuable. At his death at eighty-three in 1877, 90 percent of his $105-million fortune was from the railroad business.

Three men—Steven Girard, John Jacob Astor, and Cornelius Vanderbilt—were among the richest men ever to make their fortunes in America. The importance of their wealth came not from its size at the time of their death, but the relative amount of that wealth as compared to the wealth of others. These men, each for a while called the richest in the country, were vastly richer than the other rich. Their wealth enabled them to control far more resources than anyone else could. They made all of their money themselves—none inherited anything or had much help in getting started. They were uneducated, roguish entrepreneurs, driven to be tough competitors at a time when American capitalism was in its most savage stage. They had no social graces or connections. Each had seized an opportunity unique to his time—Girard in navigation when it was badly needed, Astor in commerce by organizing the huge American fur trade (which was perhaps the first American business to spread across the continent, and for which the markets were global). And Vanderbilt was on the scene when the country's need for waterborne and rail transportation was critical, and he controlled much of the supply of ships and trains. As devoted as each was to his principal business, each traded it later in life to dominate a second business, from which each made most of his fortune.

The second half of the nineteenth century was one of America's most sustained periods of economic growth. After the Civil War, the country settled down to the extraordinary tasks of settling the West, expanding railroad networks across the country, and building its first "national" industries in coal and steel, chemicals, foodstuffs, timber, and mining. This was a period of intense transformation of the American economy from a predominantly agricultural one into a predominantly industrial one, and few laws or regulations existed to impose order and fairness on the process. Legislative bodies were not responsive to the larger questions of the times; many representatives were easily corrupted or part of political machines designed only to maintain power and collect spoils. Throughout the country, railroads and other large businesses were known to buy the compliance of state and municipal bodies in schemes of their own. Perhaps the best that can be said of this rough, raucous, money-mad period is that the same rules applied to all the players. Virtually all of the men of great wealth who emerged during this time did not begin with any advantages other than the opportunities that were presented and their own determination.

This was the time of the great American *nouveaux riches*. In 1892, the *New York Tribune* published a list of over four thousand millionaires, more than a hundred of whom had fortunes exceeding $10 million. It was also estimated that 9 percent of the population controlled 71 percent of the national wealth. Huge fortunes were made during this period, and many of them were squandered on incredible trophy-mansions and lavish living. The rich flaunted their money, eager for all to see it.

The most popular writer of his day was Horatio Alger, who died in 1899. Alger sold more than 20 million copies of cheap paperback novels to men and boys throughout the country seeking reassurance that hard work, pluck, and virtuous living would be rewarded with riches and fame. Young men starting with nothing could aspire to having it all. Alger, like Benjamin Franklin before him, had a following, not because his books were of literary excellence (they weren't), but because he touched on people's ambition to rise above their starting point. Their dreams in the later part of the nineteenth century were to get rich. Indeed, this was possible only in the great and bountiful land of opportunity that was America.

Up until the recession of 1893–97, the emerging captains of industry and finance were almost deified, but afterward, public opinion changed. Mark Twain in his novel *The Gilded Age,* published in 1873, viciously lampooned the era. Earlier society had marveled at the inventions, progress, and rising living standards brought on by American business. People didn't worry about how it happened, they were just glad that it did. Then, in the gloom of the recession that brought unemployment levels to higher than 20 percent in New York City, violent labor strikes across the country, and the march of "Coxey's Army" of unemployed to Washington to seek relief, the "Progressive Era" began. Journalists known as "muckrakers" exposed the unseemly business practices of the rich and chastised them for their avarice, self-indulgence, and lack of social responsibility. Congress investigated many of these practices and initiated moves to redistribute national income. An income-tax law was passed in 1894, but later struck down by the Supreme Court.[11] Another attempt, in 1913, resulted in an amendment to the Constitution to allow the income tax.

Matthew Josephson wrote a well-balanced history of this time of corporate agglomerators and rogues, extending from after the Civil War until the battle for control of the Northern Securities Corporation (another railroad campaign) in 1901. His book *The Robber Barons,* first published in 1934, was written during the Great Depression, when President Hoover's "era of the new prosperity had ended and its captains and kings of industry had departed." He described the times, the events, and the people of the "Gilded Age," focusing particularly on five giants of the period: Andrew Carnegie, Jay Cooke, Jay Gould, J.P. Morgan, and John D. Rockefeller. They were the great business and financial figures of the late nineteenth century, some of them perhaps among the greatest of all times. They lived in an age of new economic frontiers, when standards of the marketplace were not high, nor were there laws to enforce them. Often they presented the rough face of capitalism in its rawest form, but they were not all bad. Many were deeply religious, many contributed more generously to churches, universities, hospitals, and cultural institutions than their European counterparts ever had. Such good works were appreciated and acclaimed. Some were pillars of "respectable" society. We may look back on it as an ugly time, but for most of it, the barons were looked up to as heroes. While their riches may have been earned with little regard for social equality (as is almost always the case), and they may have been bullies or rogues of a sort, they were, for the most part, self-made men whom many Americans aspired to be like.

By 1900, the United States had begun to resemble the great economic power that Adam Smith predicted. It was then a vast, richly endowed, self-governed nation of 76 million people. It was the largest economy in the world, and the largest manufacturing nation. Its enormous efforts in taming a wilderness and giving birth to mighty new industries were governed almost entirely by what Adam Smith would have been happy to call laissez-faire economic policies, but others would call unscrupulous, barefisted free enterprise. Even so, Adam Smith would have been proud. The economic potential of America, in which he had expressed such confidence, had proven successful. Better than that, much of Adam Smith's own democratic, free-enterprise model was in place, which was more than could be said for Great Britain before 1850. In America, there was a functioning and fair judicial system (at least for whites). Few federal monopolies or exclusionary regulations existed. Market prices were set by the interaction of supply and demand. Few laws or regulations impeded profitable investments, but there were risks galore. These risks attracted men and women who wanted to follow their self-interest and develop their abilities as fully as they might. They were immigrants, settlers, shippers, and financial operators betting their capital on a favorable outcome.

CHAPTER 5

NOTHING LIKE IT IN THE WORLD

American enterprise has now survived for more than two and a quarter centuries, and rather than fading away to make room for a more dynamic economy elsewhere, it remains a model for, and the envy of, the world. Indeed, this model, which marries the essential principles of American democracy with those of the free market, is still both unique and successful. Stephen Ambrose referred to the transcontinental railroad system (completed in 1868) as an achievement so significant that "there was nothing like it in the world," but the same could be said for the American free-enterprise system, an achievement of even greater and more lasting significance.

By the end of the twentieth century, many other countries had altered their system of political economy to adapt an American-style form of free-market capitalism in order to benefit from the economic growth that such a system can provide. Europe has, for the first time in history, transformed itself into a fledgling but promising economic union of states. The former Soviet Union imploded because of economic failure, and Russia is trying to refashion itself into some sort of nonsocialist market economy. And Latin America and Southeast Asia are also trying to move their ineffective postcolonial economic systems forward into more market-oriented policies. A number are finding success in doing so.

There are persistent criticisms of the seemingly cold, harsh characteristics of laissez-faire that are thought to illuminate a particularly American indifference to economic inequality. But the criticisms are abated by generally wide acceptance of the fact that high-growth economies produce more wealth and a more equitable distribution of it, less unemployment, and less waste of public monies, than do socialist-oriented economies. The proof of the validity of the system is in its acceptance not only by the former communists, socialists, and mixed-economy regions of the world that have taken steps to emulate the American system, but also by the continuing human and investment migration to America, which flows as eagerly as it has for more than two hundred years.

Looking back, we can say that the unique American

enterprise system derives from several connected parts of its history that were hammered into place during the first thirty years of the new republic. These were the most crucial years in terms of the nation's survival, after which, as Jefferson said, the pattern of the economic system itself had hardened and "become permanent." There was nothing like it in the world. There still isn't.

The constituent parts were unique to the American experience. First there was the relatively classless, self-improving colonial population that prospered by hard work and endurance for a hundred and fifty years. We see plenty of traces in our culture today of the rugged frontiersman, the entrepreneurial merchant, and the sharp Yankee trader, together with the more genteel tobacco planter, who built the colonial economy in those years. Benjamin Franklin openly encouraged those at the bottom of the economic ladder—apprentices and recent immigrants—to aspire to affluence, which he assured them they could achieve if they were energetic, enterprising, and frugal. Many did succeed, and their stories encouraged others. Among the numerous accomplishments of Franklin, we might add the first baiting of the lure that attracted so many to America in the years following the Revolution to improve their position in life.

Next came the decision by a group of colonists to seek independence from British rule, itself an unthinkably dangerous and unlikely proposition at the time. What was it about the colonial Americans that inspired them to do this? They had carved out a generally self-governed, relatively prosperous economic society that was more equitable and offered more opportunity for self-improvement than was to be had in the mother country. Most of the American colonists were better off economically than they would have been had they lived in England. They were incensed not by the taxes collected to provide for their defense— they had voluntarily paid such taxes, which they assessed on themselves (after some bickering with the British) during the French and Indian War. Probably they would have agreed to continue to pay for the defense of the frontier after that war, as long as the decision to do so was left for them to make. Their principal objection was to the British imposition of taxes on America in order to defray expenses of *maintaining the British Empire elsewhere,* a kind of tenant-farmer relationship with an absentee landlord.

The colonists objected to the high-handed and arrogant ways the British employed to enforce the decisions of king and Parliament, which Americans (and some British) believed were contrary both to the English constitution and the mother country's long-term interests. America's expression of opposition unleashed harsh, ill-considered efforts by the British to impose their taxes and other programs on the country, but the colonists patiently resisted the use of force in protest. Ultimately, however, they sought to be free of the British once and for all, though perhaps at that time, as many as two-thirds of the colonial population would rather not have gone that far. The revolutionaries gathered what talent they could—an assemblage of inspirational politicians, amateur soldiers, and resourceful merchants—to prosecute a revolution to protect what they insisted were their rights. No other colony in the world was then thought to have any rights at all. No other English-speaking colony had them at the time, nor has one since ever put forth a revolution to secure them.

The Americans organized a Continental Congress representing each of the thirteen independent colonies, and all major actions had to be approved by the elected legislature of each colony. The American Revolution was not a *coup d' état*; it was an orderly process using legal measures to affect a separation from Britain. All those years of self-sufficient management under a light British hand (before 1750) had produced a special breed of hardy, self-confident individuals who could be pushed only so far. They wanted to be rid of the British and the British king, but they did not seek to overturn their own government, i.e., their legislatures and Congress. It was secession, not the sort of revolution that the French experienced in the next decade (and the Russians did in 1917), in which the people took over and forcefully ousted the established upper classes. And (as also occurred in the case of the secession of the southern states in 1861) the American secession was organized and executed by its society's leading people. These were the men and women who pledged their lives, fortunes, and sacred honor, knowing that all of these might be lost. They had the courage and the pluck—these colonial farmers, merchants, planters, and frontiersmen—to pull away from their harsh and lordly parent. Nothing like it had ever happened before.

But no matter how honorably motivated they were, the rebels still had to win the war, or, as Franklin quipped, they would "all hang together" for having tried but failed. Most historians believe that from the outset, Washington's forces had little chance of winning battles, only in wearing the British down and raising the cost to them of the effort to suppressing the revolution. There was much opposition to Britain's American policies in London, and both sides perhaps hoped for a negotiated settlement of some kind after a year or two of skirmishing. Not many European states believed that the Americans had much chance of success despite the frequent errors and fumbling of the British. It was two and a half years into the war before the American victory at Saratoga (a British failure of communications probably caused the defeat) finally brought France (with its own agenda) into the war on the American side. Then came the stunning events that led to the concluding victory at Yorktown, a hundred-to-one shot at best.

After the battle, the British had to face the fact that the War of American Independence (their term), which had already cost £100 million ($12 billion in today's dollars), would cost even more if they chose to replenish the troops that had just surrendered at Yorktown. Could it be worth it? The cost and the failures at Saratoga and Yorktown were wearing down the national will in Britain to continue the war. The strength of the opposition party, which opposed the war in order to oppose the party in power, finally gathered enough support in March 1782 to gain a majority and topple the government. However, the very next month, Admiral de Grasse's enormous French fleet, without which the victory at Yorktown could not have been possible, was soundly defeated by the British in an important naval battle in the Caribbean, the Battle of the Saints. This victory stiffened the British backbone, and the subsequent peace negotiations with the colonists were dragged out for another year and a half and were never easy.

In America, there was great objection to the terms of the treaty when they were published. But even then, the British (i.e., the replacement government, which had opposed the war) held back on implementing the treaty. They kept troops in place in the Great Lakes region, continued to disallow American trade, and harassed the country's shipping. They attempted to isolate the new republic, hoping to force it into internal chaos sufficient to give themselves another chance to recoup their losses—either by voluntary submission should the republic fail (as the Commonwealth was followed by the restoration of the monarchy after the death of Oliver Cromwell), or by military conquest.

In 1812, the British tried again militarily, and though technically they won the key battles (they occupied and burned the city of Washington), the war ended in a stalemate, largely because of several successful American naval battles and Andrew Jackson's rout of the British army at New Orleans. No matter how it had come out, however, the British could not have occupied the country militarily. This would have involved great cost in men and money, and they were still fighting Napoleon's armies in Europe. Thus the Americans had certainly made one point clear—that unless a foreign army was prepared to occupy the country and control every inch of it, it could not rule American land or its people. Economically, it made no sense for any European power to attempt such a monumental task (though Napoleon considered it briefly). By 1815, it was all over. Napoleon was gone and the British were content to work with the Americans rather than against them. Henceforth no one could ever govern Americans but themselves.

But how would they do so? They tried confederation first, but the experiment was a failure and led to the Constitutional Convention; that the confederation had failed was the one and only thing the first attendees agreed on. But what should they have in its place? Ideas were put forward and debates held. The debates lasted for more than two years, not very long considering the importance of the subject and the amount of ground to be covered, but time was short. Guided by Hamilton, Jay, and Madison, a constitution finally emerged, one distinguished by the limits it placed on any sector of government from gaining power over the others. We call them "checks and balances," but they were a series of vetoes that allowed a federal system to be effective only if it could gather wide support from all three independent branches of government. The genius of the document was in creating power by denying it.

The Constitution, of course, was only as good as those who had to put it into effect and defended it. Changes or amendments to constitutions are common in most countries that have them; often they are amended beyond recognition. Also, the way in which constitutions are interpreted, and by whom, can determine great issues of power concentration and distribution. George Washington might have decided to stay in office indefinitely, based on the well-intended advice of his supporters that the country would fall apart otherwise. He might have acted on that advice and decided to remain as President for the rest of his life, setting a very different precedent from what he actually did. He also might have used his enormous popularity (which grew every time people thought the country was in trouble) to put through a few constitutional amendments of his own choosing. He might have felt it necessary to retain the support of Congress, cabinet officers, or wealthy citizens in general by rewarding them with patroon-like land grants, a practice common in just about every other country Washington and the rest of his cabinet knew of. Enfranchisement might have been restricted over time, rather than widened. The support of state governors might have had to be assured by grants of land or favors, a practice that would have to be maintained indefinitely, as in the European feudal systems in order to maintain the balance of power between king and barons. A great deal could have gone wrong with the Constitution, and might very well have but for one thing: The early officeholders respected it and did not want to amend it more than was absolutely necessary.

The first ten amendments were adopted along with the Constitution itself as the *Bill of Rights*. The Eleventh Amendment related to the judiciary, and the Twelfth to the process of selecting the President and vice-president; they were passed in 1795 and 1804 respectively. But the next amendment, the Thirteenth, was not approved until 1865. Out of regard for American democracy (and because he claimed to be tired of the office), Washington declined to run after a second term and never sought any privileges or a position of nobility. (Compare him to Napoleon Bonaparte, who crowned himself emperor in 1804). The Constitution became a constant in American governance, a bulwark on which all could agree. It distributed power rather than consolidated it, and it became the centerpiece of all the key American institutions—the legal system, the military, the economy, and the system of protections of individual rights.

The Constitution itself had many effects on American enterprise. The states would retain the power to create corporations and to regulate intrastate commerce, thereby greatly decentralizing it. When matters of interstate commerce arose, however, the federal government could step in to resolve disputes or establish policies to avoid them. Federal government intervention could take place only by legislation, which was subject to judicial review of its constitutionality, or by executive order, which could be overturned at the polls. The guiding constraints were that government laws and actions could not deprive citizens of their constitutional rights, including the right to fairness and a level playing field. All this helped set American commerce and industry off on a footing that favored open competition in the marketplace and limited government intervention on behalf of market participants.

The Constitution also gave powers to the federal government to negotiate international trade agreements, impose tariffs (by legislation), and to spend money on national defense, which for most of the nineteenth century meant the protection of maritime trade and American shipping. All of these measures were important to a new nation with fledgling industries and an entirely new commercial and trade system to develop.

The Constitution also gave power to the government to

establish a monetary system and to regulate the nation's finances. No other power was more important to the development of enterprise than that which affected the value of the currency and the credibility of the financial system. No task of government was more difficult to implement effectively. The job fell to Alexander Hamilton, and in retrospect, we have to be amazed at how well he handled it. He defined a new currency, the U.S. dollar, and called for a mint to coin it. He consolidated the national debt and set up funds to amortize it, giving rise to American securities markets. He established the Bank of the United States, which, as the country's central bank, could set about building a competent national banking system. He encouraged manufacturing as a future source of economic growth and national economic independence, and he supported a strong national defense. He was an activist and a fiscal conservative who believed that a strong central government was necessary for these objectives, but he also wanted a strong federal government able to exert itself frequently and extensively in the interest of promoting projects of national importance.

Not having been born or raised in a state, Hamilton cared little for states' rights. He was indisputably brilliant and saw most things in the perspective of a practical man of affairs with little time for abstract nuances. He and Jefferson almost drove each other crazy, but each was the other's intellectual and political equal and their conflicts were not unexpected. Hamilton set the country on a sound economic and financial footing that has stood the test of time.

There is also the piece of American entrepreneurial history that is rooted in immigration and foreign investment. The people and the money came to America because the system was seen to work fairly from the very beginning. It offered opportunity for ordinary people to find a new life, and opportunity for wealthy investors looking for greater returns in an environment of growth amidst comparative financial stability. The world's first sniff of effective democratic, free-market capitalism brought an enormous response, and it still does.

And finally, there was the Industrial Revolution in America. In a short period of time, it enabled manufacturers to shift the economy away from agricultural dominance and to raise the standard of living enjoyed by the majority of citizens. The technological developments increased factory utilization and improved productivity, which shortened the workday, raised wages, and encouraged universal education, which in turn increased knowledge and brought about even newer technologies. It also increased urbanization and the need for transport to bring farm goods to the cities. In America, whole new markets were being developed—because of new things to sell, more people to sell them to, and more once-remote locations in which to do it. These growing markets offered economies of scale to manufacturers, who were able to lower prices further as a result. By the end of the nineteenth century, the American economy had emerged as the world's most powerful.

The country owes great debts of gratitude to its founding fathers, particularly to Washington and Hamilton, but also to Jefferson and Gallatin, as well as a long succession of others in high office, who have preserved the essential American principles of enterprise for over two hundred years.

When we look to trace the origins of these essential principles, we must save some credit for Adam Smith, the reclusive Scottish academic who never visited America, who was loyal to the British government despite policies of which he disapproved, and who died before the new American government was more than two years old. *The Wealth of Nations* was read by many constitutional framers and by George Washington, whose copy of the 1789 edition bearing his signature is now retained by the Firestone Rare Book Library at Princeton. Certainly Alexander Hamilton, the country's first financial executive and son of a Scotsman, read it, for he often quoted Smith and tried to distinguish his policies from those of his better-known countryman, Jefferson, who was familiar with Smith's work and favored his agricultural prejudices. Franklin was a friend of both David Hume and the French *philosophes* and very aware of Smith. Madison and Adams were, too, but no one ever claimed to have followed a Smithian blueprint in constructing the country's economic system. Hamilton indeed rejected Smith's principle of free trade in order to protect the budding industry in America, and he was probably too proud to admit to following the abstract ideas of a distant, now-dead philosopher in attempting to construct his new country's policy priorities.

Alexander Hamilton was a practical man of action who believed that only those with the greatest worldly experience—those whose personal actions were the most admirable—should be followed by others. Hamilton believed in deal-making through compromise and maneuver, which of course is how politicians govern. Parts of Hamilton's 1791 *Report on Manufactures* are extended criticisms of Adam Smith's essentially laissez-faire views of the role of government. Hamilton wanted a strong central government to promote industrial development actively, and with subsidies if necessary. His efforts reflected not only his policy preferences, but the fact that the subject of the policies was a brand-new republic with no existing laws, traditions, or practices to obstruct progress. America certainly was not Britain in 1798.

Adam Smith's deductive recommendations were focused on Britain's economic system; he was not offering advice to America, but to Britain, and his advice might have been very different had he been. Peter McNamara, an American political scientist, wrote about the roles of Smith and Hamilton in the foundation of the American "commercial republic" and concluded that the main differences between the two were only of method. Smith was addressing what a political economy ought to look like if one focused only on its lasting objective (the maximization of opulence); Hamilton was interested only in creating a system that would work—i.e., create some opulence—for America in the here and now. In general, Hamilton thought Adam Smith's reasoning was correct, though he judged him mainly on what he thought was useful to America. Though Britain and America had totally different systems, Adam Smith's universal ideas were thought to apply for the most part to the young country and the old.

Thomas Jefferson, on the other hand, seemed more easily to warm up to Smith. Both men claimed to recognize the economic and moral supremacy of agriculture. Both claimed to want to see a light-handed government that would not interfere in the natural order of things—i.e., the country's markets and customs—or be greedy in presuming economic powers for itself, a policy both correctly assumed Hamilton was guilty of doing. Jefferson, wearing his sometime mantle as a gentle philosopher and admirer of the Enlightenment, would approve Smith's claim that no economic system that was not "just" could long prevail, but Jefferson had to offset that view with his tolerance of slavery, a practice that Hamilton, an early abolitionist, did not share. Hamilton was more pragmatic than Jefferson, especially in his insistence on a strong national defense, a stable currency (based on debt consolidation and reduction), and a central bank. However, Jefferson could be pragmatic, too. He not only allowed Hamilton's policies to remain in effect when he became President; he took on a major concession to federalism in agreeing to spend federal money on the Louisiana Purchase, ostensibly to improve trade. Hamilton, then a Federalist in opposition, grumbled that the acquisition was an important one but the land would not have much value for many years and it probably would have been cheaper to take it by force than to pay Napoleon for it.[1] One suspects, however, that if the opportunity had been presented five years earlier, Hamilton would have seized on it as quickly as Jefferson did.

Adam Smith's legacy stands by itself, not in comparison to statesmen of his own or later times. It does so because like legacies of all seminal thinkers, it established a new way of thinking about something important—in this case, economics. Smith's basic idea (stretched and simplified a little to ensure its original properties) was that to gain the most wealth, the entire economic system must function in *free* markets. He was familiar with the work of other Enlightenment figures delving into social thought, ethics, and even mathematics, and his ideas carry themes observed elsewhere—in Hume, in the Marquise de Condorcet, and others of the French *philosophes*. But Smith went where they did not, into the wider realm of political economics and the design of a program for economic governance with a single object: the creation of maximum national wealth, from whence came all power and collective well-being.

And when he advanced this theory, Smith deduced (there was no "evidence" to collect and so he just thought it up) that the most efficient system was one in which government influence was withdrawn in favor of market forces. This was radical thinking for his time. There were no such economic systems in existence, and there was little support in the pragmatic world that such a system could work.

Smith's thoughts indeed reflected some of the stardust of the Enlightenment to those who were involved in it, but few men of affairs took it very seriously. William Pitt was one who did, but he was out of office and semi-retired by then. Though the Industrial Revolution, with its insatiable demand for cheap factory labor, shook up things in England and drove its economy into a realm that Smith had not foreseen, the final liberalization of the British economy did not begin for at least forty years after Smith had died.

While the British take full credit for him, Smith's appeal was at best an export commodity whose influence was greatest outside Britain. He was praised by a few contemporary scholars, but when the French Revolution came, an event greatly feared and deplored in British higher society, his work was seen to have been encouraging it. Smith's friend David Hume, an iconoclast to many in Britain, named him in his will as his literary executor for some of his more controversial writings, and Hume's disreputable reputation served to contaminate Smith's reputation as well. When Smith died, it was little noticed in England, or even in Scotland. Public obituaries were brief and often disparaging. The *Annual Register,* Oxford Professor Emma Rothschild observed, devoted only twelve lines to Smith and sixty-five lines to Major Ray, a deputy quartermaster general who was interested in barometers. Smith was praised by the wrong people—by Condorcet, a figure of the French Revolution, and by Thomas Paine, no friend of the British and a defender in the early 1790s of the French. By 1792, Smith was being reviled even in Scotland for his seditious opinions, which were thought to be inflaming Scottish peasants to riot. In the early 1800s, his reputation attracted more scholarly defense and began to recover, though he was probably unknown outside of academia. Throughout most of the nineteenth century, he was seen as an overrated figure of liberalism, of quaint methods and reasoning, and one who stumbled around in his material, making numerous scholarly errors.[2]

Interest in Smith was rekindled when Friedrich Hayek, the twentieth-century Austrian economic philosopher (and, until Milton Friedman, reigning prince of the conservative school of economics), praised him as a precursor of "spontaneous order." This is a condition in which social institutions come into being without any advanced human intention and function well without planning or design. It is a tribute to the "invisible hand," an important principle of faith for conservatives that things will work out best if left alone. This was by no means an obvious position to take in Adam Smith's times (or later), when renowned figures such as John Maynard Keynes insisted on government economic intervention as a means to improve national performance. Smith has also been identified with the school of pro-greed apologists, because of his promotion of "self-interest as a motivator" and his advocacy of laissez-faire, which has become a poster child for inhumane, results-only capitalism. Many scholars have devoted their careers to arguing where in the spectrum of liberalism-conservatism Smith properly belongs. Emma Rothschild recently published *Economic Sentiments,* a book that attempts to restore the humane side to Smith's economic theories.

Adam Smith was a moral philosopher who turned to economics as a way to project his work into the arena of "what should be." His discovery that markets are unpredictable, and yet reflect and process economic information, has made him the veritable founding father of the economics profession. His preference for free-market forces was formed after observing how extensively negative the role of governments could be in allocating scarce economic resources. Further, Smith's observation on the corrupting influence of government involvement in the economy, in which rules were set down in order to be bribed away, tariffs imposed to protect the interests of wealthy landholders, kickbacks considered part of the compensation of officials, government and military offices made available for sale, and monopolies granted to corporations such as the East India Company to favor shareholders at the expense of the public—all these led him to believe that the less involvement by government in economic and fiscal matters, the better. Smith understood why such practices had developed and did not condemn them *per se,* but he did think they were inefficient and destroyed national wealth in favor of enriching only a few.

His theories of the greater efficiency of specialized labor and the motivational effects of self-interest have long since been vindicated by observed behavior, including the migration of 20 million people to America from Europe in the nineteenth century. His claim that an economy based on colonial mercantilism will not optimize wealth has been borne out by the collapse of the British Empire and the rise of the American noncolonial state. His recognition that economic systems must be judged as fair to work well and to last are now generally accepted. He did not believe that economic growth was a zero-sum game (in which there were only winners and losers), another new idea for his times that has been shown to be correct. Governments, he asserted, should adhere to useful activities such as providing for justice, national defense, and public works, and leave the rest to the marketplace. Of course, in Adam Smith's time, Keynesian notions of priming the pump to stimulate growth by spending government monies on public projects or welfare were unheard of, and no one seemed very concerned about reducing poverty or improving public living standards.

In our time, Smith is the symbol of economic conservatism. He is seen as cheering on policies of laissez-faire and small government, and eschewing social policies to help the poor and the weak. Having been coopted by Hayek and Friedman, he is viewed as the original champion of free-market forces and letting the chips fall where they may.

However, looked at in the context of his own place and time—Britain before the Industrial Revolution—Adam Smith would have to be seen as a lone figure attempting to preach to British politicians and aristocratic landholders a gospel of liberal economic reform. In philosophical circles, there was some interest in reforms, but not much of it was found in Buckingham Palace, the cabinet, the House of Lords, or the city of London. Smith got away with his criticisms (in the sense that his book was widely known and respected, and he was not shunned by his friends in high places) because he was not trying to revile or destroy the politics or the systems in place. His criticism was fairly light, sometimes humorous, and aimed at practices put in place long ago, for which no one living could be held accountable.

Smith had friends in the government and wanted to keep them, so he did not attack the government. *The Wealth of Nations* only pointed out that there was a better way for the country to accumulate national wealth and that everyone would be better off were it followed. But in Britain, it was not to be, at least for quite a while. The practices by which Britain's political economy was governed were too institutionalized to change quickly. Ireland was brought into union with Great Britain (and no longer continued as a colony) in 1800; the protective tariffs on wheat (called "corn" in Britain) were abolished in 1846, and the East India Company, after a series of canceled monopolies, finally was dissolved in 1857. The biggest events affecting Britain in the first half of the nineteenth century were the Napoleonic wars and the Industrial Revolution, both of which had powerful effects on future economic policies. But the policies themselves did not change much until these events forced them to.

In America at this time, a new country was being formed that would reject all the elements of colonial rule and institute new, modern, state-of-the-art economic principles so as to incorporate the most advanced, enlightened thinking of the day. Adam Smith of course came to mind, along with some of the French *philosophes* and some of the English political thinkers. America's founders, however, were not just thinkers—they were also adept at compromise and knew that they had to retain support sufficient to implement whatever system was brought forward. They were thus practical men of their times, and none of them were known to have sat down and gone through Adam Smith's *The Wealth of Nations* page by page looking for applicable lessons. But when the founders did their work, they knew that Smith's ideas were there, giving encouragement for them to think about economic principles differently than did the British. It was almost as if an invisible hand had guided the new republic into realms never anticipated or expected, but realms that were accessible only if the economy was left open and free, with a level playing field for all. Though Smith's contributions are little recorded in American history (unlike those of Locke, Hume, and Burke), the new American state was more Smithian than the old British one was. And its system of public enterprise was ready to adapt to and benefit from the huge changes in economic management that lay ahead in the nineteenth century.

Adam Smith also handed a loaded gun to the Americans in setting forth objections to British mercantilism. The Revolution got going fast and furiously before these arguments were properly grasped by more than a few of the founding fathers. Surely, however, if the Revolution had not taken place when it did—had the British resolved the disputes with the colonies amicably—it might well have taken place later over the inflexible practices and double standards of mercantilism. But even if the colonies had been restored to quiet, the British would still have had to experience the French Revolution on their doorstep and then fight Napoleon. If all that happened, chances are that the colonies would have been drawn into the war as suppliers of manufactured goods and possibly of troops. Mercantilism may have died of its own weight, as Smith implicitly suggests it was about to do. If so, perhaps the issue of separation would have been postponed indefinitely, as it was in the other principal English-speaking colonies: Canada, South Africa, Australia, and New Zealand.

Canada did not become an independent, self-governing entity until 1931. South Africa, after a referendum, became fully independent only in 1961. Australia and New Zealand, while independent states, are still part of the British Commonwealth, though Australia did not become independent of the British Parliament until 1986.

Canada in 1800 had major establishments on two seacoasts and the Great Lakes. It could grow grain to feed itself, and had access to minerals, timber, and fisheries. In 2000, Canada had a population of 31 million, and a GDP per capita of about three-quarters that of the United States.[3] Friedrich Engels, while visiting North America in 1888, found many contrasts between those on either side of the border. They had different value systems, he said, with the Canadians being more docile, more European in accepting order and hierarchy and British rule. The economic animals of the day, Engels thought, were the Americans south of the border, who shared none of these characteristics but were fiercely independent and entrepreneurial. Many Canadian writers still seem to attribute these differences to the revolutionary war, in which the winners remained in the United States but the losers moved to Canada and acted accordingly for another hundred years.[4] Would America be like Canada today if the Revolution had not occurred?

Well, the Revolution did occur, and if it had not, it might have been provoked by the need to throw off the shackles of mercantilism. Differences of character developed between the North Americans that had a lot to do with their experience of enterprise. In the United States, enterprise was needed, valued, and set free to run its course, which served it very well. The path it followed was perhaps as democratic as it could be, one in which impediments to a free market were removed in the interest of citizens' rights. Adam Smith provided a map of this pathway, a template for a free-market model that apparently was usable only by Americans, because the British were not about to adopt it, not for themselves or their colonies. So without Adam Smith, American economic development might have occurred more slowly, hindered by self-erected obstacles. It seems also that without America, Adam Smith's theories would never have had a full airing and an opportunity to be tested. But we do know this: He had the right ideas for America, and he had them at the right time. Only Americans have had a long, successful track record of following the template he sketched out, and no other country has developed such an extensive and effective system of private enterprise.

EPILOGUE

The ideas of Adam Smith helped form the model for the development of the American economy. Smith was, after all, the founding father of economics, and his writings, including *The Wealth of Nations,* were mainly aimed at policy-makers. His theories as it happened, appeared just in time to be of use to the founding fathers of America. Perhaps his main contribution was to question a number of British economic practices and policies that had been in place for more than a century and therefore had served as a example to be followed by others envious of Britain's economic success.

Smith was a source of encouragement to the inexperienced Americans to trust in their principal ideas—especially in the motivational powers of self-interest operating in a context of free markets, which Smith extolled and Alexander Hamilton and others pointed to as a justification for revolution and self-government. The Americans also looked to Adam Smith for assurance that whatever economic system they produced, it would have to be just and fair for it to operate efficiently and to endure. These principles coincided, of course, with the essential nature of a democratic republic, and therefore they fit the American political-economic model far better than the European. But even so, there had not been many successful democratic republics, and the American founders surely utilized all the ideas and encouragement they could get from well-regarded scholars of the subject. Adam Smith never blessed anything the Americans came up with—he mainly criticized the existing British practices—but he believed wholeheartedly in the long-term potential of America and undoubtedly would have been pleased to see some of his ideas put to work there.

Policies, however, are not everything. It may be that the very size of the American economic space and the speed at which it was filled during the nineteenth century were just too great for any policies—especially those of a small and unestablished federal government—to have had much effect. Also, it may be that four massive, unanticipated changes in the American political-economic landscape— the Louisiana Purchase, the Mexican War and the annexation of the western states, the California gold rush, and the Civil War—forced the economic consequences that actually occurred. Such consequences, then, would not be the result of thoughtfully laid-down principles of economic development and faithfully adhering to them over an extended time, but instead, they would simply be the natural results of an economic form of serendipity. Maybe. But only anarchists believe that policies don't matter. Policies and the ability to execute and enforce them matter a lot, particularly over a long period of time.

America's long-term economic development followed essential Smithian policies for most of its first fifty to a hundred years (longer than it followed anyone else's policies except for Hamilton's). These policies provided for opportunity for all within fair and justly administered free markets that would be enlarged by specialization of labor and powered by self-interest. There was to be minimal intervention by governments or their likely corruptible representatives, encouragement of free trade (once the country could afford to lift the tariffs a bit), central financial administration, and provision for national defense. In time, these principles became part of all that Americans took for granted and expected. They were embedded in the essential American economic fabric.

The American republic in its early years could have followed different paths—it could have reverted to monarchy as Britain did after the death of Cromwell, or become itself a colonial power, perhaps displacing Spain as the principal economic power in Central and South America. The country is today the result of mixing its experience with an evolving social philosophy that reflects the views of the majority of its citizens. Neither the gaining of the experience nor the evolution of the philosophy has been easy, but the nation has come to where it is in large measure because it has allowed free economic forces to drive it and been confident that such forces would produce a just and prosperous system.

Throughout the process of building the world's largest economy, however, there have been variations in the extent to which the principles of laissez-faire can be said to have applied. During the most crucial years in American economic development—when the checks and balances of governance were forged, from the early days of the republic until the Civil War—there was little economic regulation or control by today's standards. At the same time, the installation of a banking and financial system and the imposition of a series of relatively high tariffs to finance the government and protect manufacturing were powerful acts of government that surely would not have appealed to laissez-faire purists. But that is what the Americans did during a time that was otherwise devoted to laissez-faire policies. So, obviously, what took place was selective but powerful government interventions in the national economy for particular purposes. This was the pragmatic

Alexander Hamilton's repackaging of philosopher Adam Smith's policy ideas. The principles were fine, Hamilton thought, but what mattered was how the men in the arena would manage the daily affairs of state and handle the trade-offs.

If the nation needed to shore up finances in order to present a credible credit picture to investors, it had to redeem outstanding debts, set up a banking system and a base of government revenues. If it wanted to see a manufacturing capability develop after a century of mercantilism, it had to protect the new industries with tariffs. If it needed to protect its western borders and take the opportunity to develop westward, it needed to secure the land west of the Mississippi. Jefferson solved that problem by buying most it from Napoleon. James K. Polk took a different approach to the southwestern territory, seizing it instead from Mexico and in doing so, nearly doubling the American land area again. After the Civil War, there were efforts to stimulate the North and reconstruct the South through government spending programs, efforts that could hardly be deemed laissez-faire.

Otherwise, from the Civil War until the Spanish-American War, laissez-faire returned, launching the period of supreme free-market economic activity in which "robber barons" wandered a land immersed in greed, corruption, and immorality. However, between the Spanish War and World War I, the U.S. government powerfully reasserted itself into the economy with antitrust cases and the introduction of the income tax, though it made little effort to intervene in stimulating economic activity after the periodic "panics" that occurred. Between World War I and 1930, the role and power of government intervention fell off again, allowing for the first great stock market boom in the 1920s. The 1930s were the Depression years in which President Franklin Roosevelt intervened extensively in the economy. World War II, the Korean War, and the Cold War followed. The 1950s and 1960s were a time of high growth and nearly full employment, but also one of considerable government involvement and intervention through a variety of military and social spending programs, extensive regulatory regimes, and a major tax cut.

The 1970s witnessed the end of the Bretton Woods agreement for international monetary stability, Vietnam, Watergate, the energy crisis of 1973, high inflation rates, and the failure of many leading American corporations (including Penn Central and International Harvester)—all of which substantially decreased public trust and confidence in the power, integrity, and capability of the government.

In 1980, Ronald Reagan was elected President on a platform of a significantly lesser role for government and a tax reduction, but an increase in spending for national defense. Adam Smith, who was rediscovered by Americans at about this time, would have approved of Ronald Reagan, whose policies were consistent with Smithian prescriptions of laissez-faire, from which he was always ready to exempt spending for national defense. Of course the Reagan policies (except for defense) were just the opposite of FDR's and those who believed in the Keynesian notions popular in the 1960s claiming that a national economy can be successfully managed to maintain full employment by the skillful application of fiscal and monetary policies. British economist John Maynard Keynes may not have been well known to the American public, but FDR certainly was, and he was known for spending funds from the national treasury in bad times to create jobs and to improve the standard of living for America's lower- and middle-class populations. Any politician who followed FDR in office would have to do so through a set of similar populist promises, packaged with serious, avuncular prescriptions for fiscal responsibility. The Republicans (Nixon, Ford), who always emphasized fiscal responsibility, nevertheless were blamed for having brought scandal, malfeasance, and ineffectiveness into office, thereby decreasing the confidence the people had in the various roles of government in the first place, which played right into Reagan's hands.

Reagan's administration gained a substantial boost from the economic policy actions taken by the Carter government that preceded him. Inflation and interest rates were declining and a number of "deregulation" efforts had been started. But Reagan went farther—he talked Congress into a substantial tax cut that boosted growth and economic performance across the board, though it sowed the seeds of the federal government deficits, which, in the words of his budget director, extended "for as far out as the eye can see." This seemed irresponsible to many voters once the deficit had become nearly as large as predicted, and when Reagan's successor, George H. W. Bush, asked them to reelect him, of course they did not.

William J. Clinton came next as President, promising both fiscal responsibility and an expanded role for government in providing social services. A divided Congress that limited spending, and the polls, which favored reducing debt, led Clinton to the rare role of having to speak as a Democrat while acting as a Republican. He skillfully persuaded each of his audiences that what he really meant was what they really wanted to hear. He was uncommonly popular with voters despite a personal life that seemed more suitable for a soap opera than the corridors of power. His public attractiveness, however, may have had something to do with the performance of the economy, particularly the stock market. The Dow Jones Average grew at a compounded rate of 16 percent during the Clinton years, reaching its all-time high in 2000, the last year of Clinton's presidency.

Just as George H. W. Bush had the election to lose, and did lose it to Bill Clinton in 1992, Al Gore, Clinton's vice-president, had it to lose in 2000, and also lost it, though narrowly. Perhaps Gore seemed too liberal, too inclined to intervene in the magical Clinton economy and mess it up, or perhaps the voters saw the reversal in the market as it passed its peak and began to decline, slowly at first, then more rapidly as the Internet and technology sectors began to implode at the end of the Clinton years. Perhaps they thought an unknown, inarticulate, conservative Texas governor named George W. Bush would be a better risk. Both Bushes have had the tragic misfortune of following more colorful Presidents for whom the stock market appeared to sit up and bark. For both, the market would slump soon after they arrived, but surely neither Republican was about to call for massive government intervention in the market's free and natural forces. The second Bush was able to pass a modest tax cut early in his term, but it did not stop the stock market slide.

Then, suddenly, tragically—more than twenty years after the American economy had been threatened seriously by an international antagonist (when Iran, while holding American embassy hostages, forced oil prices sharply upward)—the two World Trade Center towers in New York City, part of the Pentagon, and three thousand lives were destroyed by Middle Eastern terrorists in September 2001, less than a year after George W. Bush was elected. Led by the new President, the government moved into action, first to pass a $40-billion recovery-and-relief bill, then a $15-billion airline-bailout bill, and various increases in spending for airport and national security, and for defense. Everyone approved. The country (the people and their industries) needed its government to protect it again, and to defeat its enemies.

Adam Smith would have been puzzled by all these events. National defense was a good and proper expenditure of national resources, Smith thought, and perhaps other things were too in a bona fide emergency that might threaten essential economic activity. He would have been uneasy about industry bailouts or subsidies of any type, and he certainly would be shocked by the sense of entitlement that the population as a whole seemed to have for government assistance and its tolerance of extensive regulation. Undoubtedly he would think that opulence would be impaired by such a high degree of subsidies and the regulatory costs that would inevitably drag down economic growth.

Americans clearly are ambivalent about government intervention in their economic life. Some actions are required in all times, such as maintaining a sound financial system and assuring social justice and the preservation of law and order, but the extent of the intervention is often disputed. There are other actions that are appropriate only some of the time—in times of emergency or war—and some that are hardly ever appropriate, such as federalizing the state educational role. There are times when taxes are higher than at other times, times when regulation is tighter, and times when government activity extends over larger areas. These matters fluctuate both in the frequency and the extent of the intervention, but also in terms of how much economic cost is associated with it. In theory, there ought to be an optimal level of intervention, in which the benefits of intervention (or nonintervention) exceed their costs to the maximum degree, and this may be what Adam Smith was searching for on his quest to maximize opulence. But these things don't stand still; times change, and so do all the elements of the equation.

Certainly during the period between 1980–2000, Americans were happy with the economic performance of the country. During this time, more wealth was created than during any other time in history, and large-scale government intervention in the economy—in such areas as public spending, taxation, industry regulation, and antitrust enforcement—was at as low a level as any American under seventy can remember. It may be that one can connect the two—minimal regulation and maximal prosperity. But this may be completely wrong. The World Trade Center disaster reminded all Americans that prosperity must be protected by airline-safety systems, efficient immigration and law-enforcement capabilities, strong police and fire departments, and an effective, quick-acting military service.

Indeed, the next period in the American economic experience may be one of greater expenditures on national defense and related government services, possibly at the expense of a higher growth rate in the economy. This may be comparable to spending money to protect one's country against nuclear attack during the Cold War, or in having the U.S. Cavalry patroling the plains to frighten off hostile Indian groups. It is the reverse of the "peace dividend," sadly, a concept that never had much of a chance. It may be with us for a long time, but in reality, it always has been—the United States has never been able to develop wealth without incurring substantial costs for the preservation of domestic security.

Adam Smith would remind us that without paying the cost of providing for our national defense (in all its modern ramifications), we could be less able to develop, or to retain, any opulence at all. On this point, Adam Smith and Alexander Hamilton, who had many points of disagreement, would have agreed fully. Of course, for years we have had arguments that American defense spending is excessive and that the funds could be better utilized either as tax reductions or to improve social programs. Like the arguments, both forms of expenditure—defense and social—will continue.

We must remember that Adam Smith put great value in the power of self-interest, the energy released by people trying to improve their economic condition by their own efforts. For this power to be maximized, Smith felt that society had to allow opportunity to be realized, for people to have the *freedom* to seek the opportunity for themselves.

For this freedom to produce optimal results, society had to allow fairness in economic and other dealings to serve as the essential organizing principle. Not privilege or entitlement, not rule by force or by caste. If everyone has an equal right to economic reward from endeavor, then wealth becomes a function of endeavor. Nothing was more radical in Adam Smith's time, nothing more American today. This is probably the most overlooked contribution of the thought and work of Adam Smith—that for opulence to be optimized, the system must contain an optimal level of social equity.

This picture of Adam Smith rebuts that of the hardnosed capitalist, whose revival and modern reputation was assured by Friederich Hayek and Milton Friedman, the purest of the pure market capitalists. Indeed, it is the real Adam Smith whose work supplies the antidote to the harshest of the Hayek-Friedman school, which may be right in claiming that economic performance is maximized by allowing full application of market forces, no matter what the damage in the short run. But this claim is thought to be too harsh for any widely enfranchised democratic society to tolerate, and thus politicians who follow the purists do so at their own risk. Adam Smith, on the other hand, was less an economic purist than a practical political economist. His policies, well understood, are useful to enlighten the pathway even today.

NOTES

CHAPTER 1

1. R. H. Campbell and A. S. Skinner, *Adam Smith,* London, Croon Helm, Ltd. 1982, p. 24.
2. Dugal Stewart, "Account of the Life and Writings of Adam Smith," in *Essays on Philosophical Subjects,* eds. W. P. D. Wrightman, J. C. Bryce, and I. S. Roth, Oxford Univ. Press, 1980.
3. Campbell and Skinner, p. 95.
4. Milton Friedman, "Adam Smith's Relevance for 1976," in Fred Glahe, ed., *Adam Smith and the Wealth of Nations, Bicentennial Essays,* Univ. of Chicago Press, 1976.
5. *Ibid,* 1982, p. 106.
6. *Ibid,* pp. 107–8.
7. C. P. Kindleberger, "The Historical Background of Adam Smith and the Industrial Revolution," in Thomas Wilson and Andrew Skinner, eds., *The Market and the State,* Oxford, Clarendon Press, 1976.
8. These and other references are from Arnold Toynbee, *Lectures on the Industrial Revolution in England,* Oxford Univ. Press, 1884.
9. *Ibid.*
10. Barbara W. Tuchman, *The March of Folly,* NY, Alfred Knopf, 1984, passim.
11. *Ibid.*
12. *Ibid,* p. 421.
13. David McCullough, *John Adams,* NY, Simon & Schuster, 2001, p. 102.

NOTES

CHAPTER 2

1. *Historical Statistics of the U.S., Colonial Times to 1957,* Washington, D.C., 1960.
2. I have referred to Stuart Bruchey, *The Roots of American Economic Growth 1607–1861,* NY, Harper & Row, 1965, for much of the reference information in this chapter.
3. Bruchey, p. 38.
4. Bruchey, p. 39.
5. *Ibid.*
6. Bruchey, p. 54.
7. Bruchey, p. 65.
8. Fred Anderson, *Crucible of War,* NY, Alfred Knopf, 2000, p. 718.

CHAPTER 3

1. Bruchey, p. 64.
2. Barbara Tuchman, *The First Salute,* NY, Alfred Knopf, 1988, pp. 5–8; 95–100.
3. Campbell and Skinner, pp. 163–166.
4. David McCullough, *John Adams,* NY, Simon & Schuster, 2001, p. 352.
5. Vincent P. Carosso, *Investment Banking in America,* Cambridge, MA, Harvard Univ. Press, 1970, p. 1.
6. Bruchey, p. 54.
7. Charles A. Beard, *An Economic Interpretation of the Constitution of the United States,* NY, Macmillan & Co. 1935, passim.
8. Charles A. Beard, passim.
9. Charles A. Beard, p. 101.
10. Bruchey, passim.
11. Richard Sylla, "Shaping the U.S. Financial System, 1690–1913: The Dominant Role of Public Finance," in Richard Sylla, Richard Tully, and Gabriel Tortella, eds., *The State, the Financial System,*

and Economic Modernization, Cambridge, England, Cambridge Univ. Press, 1999, passim.

12. Charles Royster, *Light Horse Harry Lee and the Legacy of the American Revolution,* Baton Rouge, LA, LSU Press, 1981, pp. 71–73.
13. Rowland T. Berthoff, *British Immigrants in Industrial America,* 1790–1950, NY, Russell & Russell, 1953, pp. 30–46.

CHAPTER 4

1. David McCullough, *John Adams,* NY, Simon & Schuster, 2001, pp. 505, 486–487.
2. Bruchey, p. 121.
3. Bruchey, p. 137.
4. Bruchey, p. 129.
5. Bruchey, p. 87.
6. Bruchey, pp. 143–148.
7. Ralph W. Hidy, *The House of Baring in American Trade and Finance,* Cambridge, Harvard Univ. Press, 1949, p. 52.
8. D. C. M. Platt, *Foreign Finance in Continental Europe and the USA 1815–1870,* London, Geo. Allen and Unwin, 1984, pp. 142–150 and Appendices I and III.
9. A. B. C. Whipple, *The Challenge,* NY, William Morrow, 1987, p. 14.
10. Arthur T. Vanderbilt II, *Fortune's Children,* NY, William Morrow, 1989, pp. 29–37.
11. Vanderbilt, *Op Cit.,* p. 266.

CHAPTER 5

1. Richard Brookheiser, *Alexander Hamilton—American,* NY, Free Press, 1999, p. 202.

NOTES

2. Emma Rothschild, "Adam Smith and Conservative Economics," *Economic History Review, XLV* 1, 1992.

3. Angus Maddison, *The World Economy—A Millennial Perspective,* Washington, OECD, 2001, p. 185.

4. Seymour Martin Lipset, *Continental Divide,* Routledge, Chapman and Hall, NY, 1990, pp. 1–19.

INDEX

INDEX

INDEX

INDEX

INDEX

Nixon, Richard, 207
Norman Conquest, 27
North, Lord, 39
North American Land Company, 127
North Carolina
   tobacco plantations in, 61
Northern Securities Corporation, 172

Ohio Company, 70–71
Oklahoma land rush, 153
Oliver & Thompson, 104
Otis, James, 76

Paine, Thomas, 193
Parish, David, 104, 162
Penn, William, 61–62, 84, 85
philosophes, 21, 191
Physiocrats, 19
Pilgrims, 40
Pitt, William (the elder), 39, 48, 191
Pitt, William (the younger), 51, 52
plantation economy
   in colonial America, 58–59, 59–65
   See also slavery
Platt, D. C. M., 163–64
Plymouth Rock, 40
Polk, James K., 205
Pontiac's rebellion, 70–71
Poor Richard's Almanac (Franklin), 80, 88
Pope, Alexander, 52
Potomac Company/Potomac Canal,
   128–29, 164
precious metals
   prohibited export of, 33
Principles of Political Economy (Mill), 6
*Principles of Political Economy and
   Taxation* (Ricardo), 6
Progressive Era, 172
Protestant work ethic
   and American capitalism, 81–84
Puritanism, 81, 83

Quartering Act, 45
Quesnay, François, 19

railroads
   development of, 167–68
   investment in, 165
   transcontinental railroad, 175

Raleigh, Sir Walter, 40
Ray, Major, 193
Reagan, Ronald, 206–8
religious freedom, 81–83
Report on Manufactures (Hamilton), 124,
   189, 190
Republican Party
   Jeffersonian, 117, 139
   modern, 207
Revolutionary War. *See* America
   (American Revolution)
Ricardo, David, 6
Robber Barons, The (Josephson), 172–73
Rockefeller, John D., 173
Rodney, George, 97
Roosevelt, Franklin D., 206, 207
Rothschild, Emma, 193, 194
Rousseau, Jean Jacques, 19
Russia
   free-market capitalism and, 176

Secondat, Charles-Louis de (Baron
   deMontesquieu), 19, 21
securities market, development of, 161
self-interest, Adam Smith and, 14–16
Seven Years' War. *See* French and Indian
   War
Shay's Rebellion, 104
Skinner, A. S., 51
Slater, Samuel, 132–33, 151
slavery
   in colonial America, 57, 64–65
   in post-Revolutionary America, 104,
      154–56
   See also plantation economy
Smith, Adam , *xi–xiii*, 7–10
   childhood and education, 10–12
   and the Enlightenment, 19, 21, 191
   reputation at time of death, 192–93
   and the University of Glasgow, 12,
      16–17
Smith, Adam (theories)
   ambition and self-interest, 14–16
   and America, *xiv*, 23–24, 50–51, 58,
      134, 188–96
   on banking, 122–23
   on Britain's handling of
      colonialAmerica, 37–40, 76–77,
      97–98

INDEX